MORE OLD TESTAMENT SINNERS AND SAINTS

DISCOVER 100 LITTLE-KNOWN BUT
INTRIGUING BIBLE CHARACTERS

BIBLE CHARACTER SKETCHES SERIES, BOOK 4

PETER DEHAAN

More Old Testament Sinners and Saints: Discover 100 Little-Known but Intriguing Bible Characters

Copyright © 2024 by Peter DeHaan.

Bible Character Sketches Series, book 4

All rights reserved: No part of this book may be reproduced, disseminated, or transmitted in any form, by any means, or for any purpose without the express written consent of the author or his legal representatives. The only exceptions are brief excerpts, and the cover image, for reviews or academic research. For permissions: peterdehaan.com/contact.

Unless otherwise noted, Scriptures taken from the Holy Bible, New International Version®, NIV®. Copyright © 1973, 1978, 1984, 2011 by Biblica, Inc.™ Used by permission of Zondervan. All rights reserved worldwide. www.zondervan.com The "NIV" and "New International Version" are trademarks registered in the United States Patent and Trademark Office by Biblica, Inc.™

Library of Congress Control Number: 2024903640

Published by Rock Rooster Books, Grand Rapids, Michigan

ISBNs:

- 979-8-88809-077-0 (e-book)
- 979-8-88809-078-7 (paperback)
- 979-8-88809-079-4 (hardcover)

Credits:

- Developmental editor: Julie Harbison
- Copy editor: Robyn Mulder
- Cover design: Cassidy Wierks
- Author photo: Chelsie Jensen Photography

To Jeremy Rowland

CONTENTS

Celebrating the Old Testament	1
1. Lamech (1)	5
2. Seth	8
3. Enoch (2)	11
4. Methuselah	13
5. Canaan	15
6. Nimrod	18
7. Job's Wife	21
8. Nahor (2)	23
9. Melchizedek	26
10. Eliezer (1)	29
11. Judith (1) and Basemath (1)	31
12. Deborah (1)	34
13. Er (1)	36
14. Onan	38
15. Shelah (3)	40
16. Perez	42
17. Zerah (3)	44
18. Potiphar's Wife	46
19. Potiphar	48
20. Asenath	51
21. Manasseh and Ephraim	53
22. Shiphrah and Puah (2)	56
23. Reuel (2)/Jethro	58
24. Zipporah	60
25. Gershom (1) and Eliezer (2)	62
26. Jannes and Jambres	64
27. Nadab (1) and Abihu	67

28. Eleazar (1) and Ithamar	69
29. Korah (3)	71
30. Phinehas (1)	73
31. Kozbi	75
32. Zelophehad	77
33. Achan	79
34. Ehud (1)	81
35. Abimelek (2)	84
36. Jotham (1)	87
37. Gaal	89
38. Jephthah	91
39. Micah (1)	94
40. Mahlon and Kilion	97
41. Obed (1)	99
42. Jabez	101
43. Elkanah (4)	103
44. Hannah	105
45. Peninnah	107
46. Hophni and Phinehas (2)	109
47. Eli	111
48. Jesse	113
49. Goliath	115
50. Merab	117
51. Michal	119
52. Ahimelek (1)	122
53. Doeg	124
54. Abner	126
55. Ish-Bosheth	129
56. Joab	131
57. Nathan (2)	134
58. Tamar (2)	137
59. Amnon (1)	139
60. Tamar (3)	141

61. Abiathar	143
62. Abishai	146
63. Hushai	148
64. Ahithophel	150
65. Amasa (1)	152
66. Abishag	154
67. Adonijah (1)	156
68. Sons of Korah (2)	158
69. Zadok (1)	160
70. Queen of Sheba	162
71. Agur	164
72. Lemuel	166
73. Rehoboam	168
74. Asa	170
75. Obadiah (4)	172
76. Gehazi	175
77. Zechariah (1)	178
78. Josiah (1)	181
79. Amos (1)	184
80. Hosea	186
81. Gomer (2)	188
82. Jezreel	190
83. Lo-Ruhamah	192
84. Lo-Ammi	194
85. Micah (5)	196
86. Nahum (1)	198
87. Zephaniah (1)	200
88. Obadiah (8)	202
89. Habakkuk	204
90. Shadrach, Meshach, and Abednego	206
91. Nebuchadnezzar	209
92. Belshazzar	213

93. Darius	216
94. Zerubbabel	219
95. Haggai	222
96. Zechariah (15)	224
97. Cyrus	226
98. Xerxes	228
99. Joel (13)	231
100. Malachi	233
More Old Testament Sinners and Saints for Us Today	235
Which Book Do You Want to Read Next?	238
For Small Groups, Sunday School, and Classrooms	239
If You're New to the Bible	241
Duplicate Names	244
About Peter DeHaan	263
Peter DeHaan's Books	265

Series by Peter DeHaan

40-Day Bible Study Series takes a fresh and practical look into Scripture, book by book.

Bible Character Sketches Series celebrates people in Scripture, from the well-known to the obscure.

Holiday Celebration Bible Study Series rejoices in the holidays with Jesus.

Visiting Churches Series takes an in-person look at church practices and traditions to inform and inspire today's followers of Jesus.

Be the first to hear about Peter's new books and receive updates at PeterDeHaan.com/updates.

CELEBRATING THE OLD TESTAMENT

Some Christians dismiss the Old Testament. They argue that since Jesus came to fulfill the Law and the Prophets (Matthew 5:17), what it says doesn't matter to them or their faith practices today. Other Christians embrace the Old Testament, putting it on an equal footing with the New Testament. They reason that all Scripture—both the Old and New Testaments—has merit (2 Timothy 3:16).

We should instead embrace the Old Testament for what it is and let it inform our understanding of the New Testament and the faith practices it reveals. We can most appreciate God's New Testament of Scripture from the foundation the Old Testament provides.

From this perspective, we can celebrate the Old Testament. It has two main purposes. The first is to reveal God to us. The second is to anticipate the coming Savior, Jesus.

In the Old Testament law—given to us through Moses—a mind-numbing list of things to do and not do confronts us. This is to make us right with Father God. But it's an impossible undertaking to achieve. Everyone falls short. Whether by a little or a lot, it matters not. We all miss the mark of the Old Testament's prescription (James 2:10).

Yet the Old Testament also gives us hope of the coming Savior who will offer a better way for us to approach God. It's a way everyone can realize—if they want to. It's believing in Jesus and following him as his disciple. This is so much better than a bunch of impossible-to-keep rules.

In this way, we can best read and understand the Old Testament as it anticipates and points us toward Jesus, the Messiah.

From this perspective, we'll continue the mission of *Old Testament Sinners and Saints* and explore one hundred more Old Testament characters. Many of their stories overlap, and others are hard to place on the biblical timeline. Yet we'll do our best to cover them in chronological order.

Some of these one hundred Old Testament characters provide examples to follow. We'll call these people saints, even though they're less than perfect. The Old Testament also includes a colorful list of screwups (sinners), the people who fall short and make a mess of things. We can see their lives as examples to avoid.

Several of these people share names with other biblical characters. For example, did you know there are two people named Noah in the Bible? Whenever we encounter a duplicate name, we'll add a number at the end to help us keep things straight. You can learn more about this in "Duplicate Names" in the back of the book.

As we consider these individuals on a continuum from mostly good to mostly bad, remember that all of them miss the mark of meeting God's Old Testament expectations. This points us to God's better way through Jesus, as revealed in the New Testament.

May these Old Testament sinners and saints inform you to embrace Jesus, first to become his disciple and then to live as one.

How do you view the Old Testament? Who are some of your favorite Old Testament characters? Why?

[Discover more in Acts 17:11.]

1. LAMECH (1)

The Bible lists no genealogy for Abel, so we can guess that he died before he had any children. Scripture focuses on the descendants of Seth but gives a short recitation of Cain's genealogy first (in Genesis 4). We must be careful in reading these names in Cain's line, since two names also appear in Seth's line, though they refer to different men.

Such is the case with Lamech (1). (The other name to be careful with is Enoch. Also, watch out for Methushael, not to be confused with Methuselah.)

We know little about Lamech, but two things stand out.

First, Lamech marries two women, Adah and Zillah.

This is the first time any form of the word *marriage* occurs in the Bible, and this passage is also the first reference to polygamy. Though Bible scholars often place elevated importance on the first time a word appears in Scripture, we must be careful not to connect marriage with polygamy.

The Bible merely states that Lamech married two women, but it adds no commentary. Therefore, we're wrong to take this descriptive text as approval for polygamy or as a warning against it. Notably, this may be the only time in Scripture when a man has multiple wives that doesn't result in conflict or heartache. Consider the multiple wives of Abraham, Jacob, David, Solomon, and many others. Each suffers as a result.

The other thing we know about Lamech is that he kills a man. He's the Bible's second recorded murderer, with Cain being the first.

Though we could charitably ascribe the death of this unnamed man by the hand of Lamech as self-defense, it's more likely an excessive retaliation. Lamech's justification is that the man he killed had wounded and injured him. Regardless, Lamech considers what he did to be less wrong than Cain murdering Abel out of jealousy.

We must note, however, that Lamech's killing of this man occurs prior to God giving Moses the Ten Commandments, which prohibit murder. Yet he should have been instinctively aware that murder is wrong.

When have we responded in an excessive manner to someone who wronged us? Do you think Lamech killed this man or murdered him? What is the difference?

[Read about Lamech in Genesis 4:19–24. All other mentions of Lamech in the Bible refer to Lamech (2), a descendant of Seth.]

2. SETH

The Bible tells us that Adam has many sons and daughters, but it only lists three sons by name. They are Cain, Abel, and Seth.

Most people know about Cain and Abel, with Cain killing Abel out of jealousy. He then flees his family to live in the land of Nod.

As a result, Adam and Eve effectively have no sons. One is dead, and the other is gone. Adam and Eve then have Seth. The meaning of the name Seth may be "granted," for God granted Adam and Eve another child.

He's essentially a replacement for Cain and Abel.

We may be uneasy about the reason for Seth's conception. This could be a positive development, with him being elevated as Adam and Eve's primary heir. Yet the idea that Seth's creation is merely to fill the void left by his murdered brother, Abel, is disconcerting.

Regardless, Seth is born.

Scripture notes that after Seth's birth is when Adam's many sons and daughters are born. Implicitly, this makes Seth Adam and Eve's third child.

The only other things we know about Seth are his descendants. The Bible lists the successive generations as Enosh, then Kenan, followed by Mahalalel, Jared, Enoch, Methuselah, Lamech, and Noah. Therefore, Noah follows Seth by eight generations.

What's even more significant, however, is that Luke lists Seth in the family tree of Jesus. Yes, Jesus descends from Seth.

If the circumstance regarding our conception is less than admirable, do we let it define who we are or do we rise above it? Though we don't know what our descendants will do long after we're gone, how should their potential inform what we do today?

[Read about Seth in Genesis 4:25–26 and Genesis 5:3–8. Discover more in 1 Chronicles 1:1 and Luke 3:38.]

3. ENOCH (2)

As we already noted, Enoch (1) is a descendant of Cain, whereas Enoch (2) is a descendant of Seth.

To give us some historical perspective, here are the world's first nine generations, from Adam to Noah:

Adam, Seth, Enosh, Kenan, Mahalalel, Jared, **Enoch**, Methuselah, Lamech, and Noah.

As we can see, Enoch is the great-grandfather of Noah, as well as six generations removed from Adam.

Scripture tells us one detail about Enoch, and it's significant.

Enoch does not die.

He walks faithfully with God and is taken up

into heaven. We can connect his faithful walk with the fact that he bypasses death and goes directly to eternity.

Enoch is the first person in the Bible to be affirmed for his faithful walk with God. Though it would be wrong to conclude that everyone who walks faithfully with God will skip death, moving directly from physical life on earth to eternal life in heaven, in this case it did happen.

Though Enoch is the first person to experience this, he isn't the last. Later, Elijah will also be taken up into heaven. These two events foreshadow the resurrected body of Jesus ascending into heaven.

What should we do to walk faithfully with God? Why should we want to do this?

[Read about Enoch in Genesis 5:18–24. Discover when Elijah is taken up into heaven in 2 Kings 2:1–11.]

4. METHUSELAH

Methuselah is Enoch's son. Aside from being Noah's grandfather, the other notable fact about Methuselah is that he has the longest recorded life in the Bible, standing at an amazing 969 years. The Bible records many people at that time as living hundreds of years, but Methuselah's life is the longest.

Yet as we move further away from the time of sin entering the world, we see life spans decreasing in length. Death, after all, is the result of sin.

Moses later places a typical person's life at seventy years, even up to eighty (Psalm 90:10). This is despite the fact that he lived to be 120 years old (Deuteronomy 34:7), which God established during the time of Noah (Genesis 6:3).

Accepting the lifespan of Old Testament characters as literal, as I do, we can determine that Methuselah—and his son Lamech (2)—are both born while Adam is still alive. They are also alive when Noah is born. This means that Methuselah and Lamech know both Adam and Noah.

Also, their lives end about the time of the flood. Did they die prior to the flood, or did they drown in the deluge?

Regardless, they were both certainly alive one hundred years earlier when God told Noah to build the ark. At that time God noted the wickedness of humanity and their persistent evil thoughts.

We're left to wonder if this critical assessment of the world's persistent evil includes Methuselah and Lamech. Regardless, Noah found God's favor (Genesis 6:1–8).

What is our view of living a long life? Whether we have days left or decades, what can we do to make every moment count?

[Read about Methuselah in Genesis 5:21–27. Discover more in 1 Chronicles 1:3 and Luke 3:37.]

5. CANAAN

Canaan is the son of Ham and the grandson of Noah. The story of Canaan is perplexing. When Noah's son Ham finds his father drunk, he acts disrespectfully. His two brothers act appropriately.

When Noah discovers what his sons did when he was inebriated, he explicitly blames Ham's son Canaan. This is despite Canaan not having any role in what happened.

We're left to wonder if we don't know the full story or if Noah reached the wrong conclusion. Nevertheless, Noah proclaims curses on Canaan.

This doesn't seem right or fair, but it is what happens.

We later read of the nations that descend from

Canaan. He is the father of Sidon and the Hittites, Jebusites, Amorites, Girgashites, Hivites, Arkites, Sinites, Arvadites, Zemarites, and Hamathites.

Although these last five nations receive scant mention in Scripture, the others reoccur.

The Sidonians (descendants of Sidon), show up 14 times.

The Hittites, 36 times.

The Jebusites, 30 times.

The Amorites, 77 times.

The Girgashites, 7 times.

The Hivites, 23 times.

Scripture reveals that these nations rise in opposition to God's chosen people, the Israelites. And this continues throughout much of the Old Testament.

We're left wondering if their opposition is a result of Noah's curse on his grandson. What if Noah had not proclaimed curses on Canaan and his descendants? Might the history in the Old Testament have unfolded differently?

Though Noah proclaimed curses on Canaan, this is not an example for us to follow. Instead, we should embrace the New Testament perspective and not curse others.

How do we respond when we're blamed for something we didn't do? What can we do to rise above any mistakes our parents might have made?

[Read about Canaan in Genesis 9:18–27 and Genesis 10:15–18. Discover more about curses in Luke 6:28, Romans 12:14, and James 3:9–10.]

6. NIMROD

Nimrod is the son of Cush, the son of Ham. Since Cush and Canaan are brothers, this means Nimrod is Canaan's nephew.

The biblical text tells us little about Nimrod. What we do know is he's a "mighty hunter before the Lord" (Genesis 10:8–9). Though this is curious wording, we can understand "before the Lord" to mean "in God's sight" or that God noticed Nimrod's hunting prowess. What's unclear is if this is a result of God's blessing on Nimrod or not.

Regardless, Nimrod establishes a kingdom, first in Babylon and then in Assyria, where he builds the city of Nineveh. Do these three locations sound familiar? Babylon appears 299 times in the Bible, Assyria 132 times, and Nineveh, twenty-six times. These mentions are as the enemy of God's chosen people, sometimes representing evil.

Parallel to the offspring of his Uncle Canaan, Babylon and Assyria also oppose God's promised people and the nations of Israel and Judah.

Assyria will later conquer the nation of Israel and deport its people. In this way, Assyria serves as God's instrument of judgment against his rebellious children.

Not learning from this example, Judah will later suffer much the same consequence. Babylon conquers Judah and deports its people too. Unlike Israel, however, some people from Judah will return to the promised land seventy years later and get a second chance. The people of Israel and Judah tested God's patience and eventually received the punishment they deserved.

In what ways do we test God's patience like the nations of Israel and Judah did? How do we react when God gives us a second chance?

[Read about Nimrod in Genesis 10:8–12. Discover more in 2 Kings 25:1–26.]

7. JOB'S WIFE

We don't know the name of Job's wife. She's a minor character in the Bible's account of his life, so we could view her name as unimportant.

Through no fault of Job, Satan attacks him, wiping away his wealth and killing all his children. Next, Satan afflicts Job's health, leaving him in agony. The suffering man wishes he were dead, that he'd never been born. All Job has left is his life, four unsupportive friends, and a wife who harasses him.

As Job struggles to maintain his faith in God and hold on to his righteousness, Job's wife could choose to support him. She should encourage him. Instead, she turns on him. She ridicules his integrity and suggests he just curse God so he can die.

A supportive wife she is not. Her reaction to his pain suggests apathy toward him, even disdain.

At a time when Job seeks comfort and encouragement from those around him, his wife lets him down. She could have—she should have—encouraged him to stand firm in his faith, to not waver or doubt. She doesn't. Instead, she urges him to give up and die.

Despite this, Job doesn't waver. He calls her foolish and does not sin. God spares Job and restores what Satan took from him.

Do we encourage those closest to us when they go through tough times, or do we make things even harder for them? How can we better support those who struggle?

[Read about Job's wife in Job 2:9–10. Discover more about a good wife in Genesis 2:18 and Proverbs 31:10–31.]

8. NAHOR (2)

There are two men in the Bible named Nahor, and they are related.

Nahor (1) is the *father* of Terah and the grandfather of Abram.

Nahor (2) is the *son* of Terah and brother of Abram and Haran.

Of Terah's three sons, Haran dies early in life, Abram goes to Canaan, and Nahor stays home. We'll circle back to him in a bit.

Terah sets out for Canaan with his nephew Lot (Haran's son), Abram, and Abram's wife Sarai. Yet Terah doesn't complete his journey. He stops midway at Harran. When Terah dies, God calls Abram to complete what his father failed to finish.

Abram, Sarai, and Lot set out for Canaan and reach it.

Much later, Abram and Sarai (then known as Abraham and Sarah) seek a suitable wife for their son Isaac. Abraham sends a trusted servant back to his relatives to find his son a bride.

Once there, Abraham's servant finds Rebekah. She's the sister of Laban, the daughter of Bethuel, and the granddaughter of Nahor—Abraham's brother.

This means that Rebekah is Isaac's first cousin once removed. Though we may shudder at the idea of marrying a close relative, God has not yet prohibited the practice, so the pair do nothing wrong by marrying.

What is notable is that God guided the servant to find Nahor's family and confirmed that Rebekah was to be Isaac's wife. Rebekah agrees and leaves with the servant.

In all of this, Nahor does nothing to make these events happen, yet without him they wouldn't have occurred.

How might God be working in our lives to bring about his

plan? In what ways might we have opposed him or cooperated with him?

[Read about Nahor in Genesis 11:26–27. Discover more in Genesis 24:15–24.]

9. MELCHIZEDEK

The mysterious character of Melchizedek shows up only once in the book of Genesis. There he meets and blesses Abraham after the patriarch defeats Lot's captors and liberates his nephew, the rest of the town, and their possessions. Abraham gives Melchizedek a tenth of the plunder.

Yet this seemingly straightforward story also intrigues.

First, Melchizedek means "king of righteousness." Next, he's a priest of God Most High. This is the Bible's first mention of a priest, so it must be significant. Third is that Salem—his kingdom—means "peace." Interestingly, the city of Salem occurs nowhere else in the Bible except in this passage regarding Melchizedek.

Therefore, we see Melchizedek as a priest and the king of righteousness who rules in peace. We must consult the book of Hebrews in the New Testament for additional insight.

Hebrews states that Melchizedek has no father or mother, no genealogy, and lives eternally without beginning or end. Therefore, he remains a priest forever with a never-ending priesthood. And he resembles the Son of God. His characteristics parallel Jesus. Some think that Melchizedek is, in fact, Jesus or at least he personifies the Messiah.

Though Jesus physically has a mother and a father, spiritually he has no genealogy. He lives eternally with no beginning or end. Through his death and resurrection, he remains a priest forever, in the order of Melchizedek (Psalm 110:4).

Moses institutes the idea of God's people having priests, but it doesn't start with Moses's brother Aaron. Melchizedek is the Bible's first mention of a priest, occurring four centuries earlier. Melchizedek precedes God's priestly line through Aaron.

There's also the tithe, a gift of ten percent. Moses also institutes the practice of the tithe, but Scripture's first mention of giving a tenth occurs here, with Abraham giving ten percent to Melchizedek. Abraham tithes to Melchizedek long before Moses commands it.

Jesus is a priest like Melchizedek, who both precedes and transcends the law of Moses.

What do you think about Melchizedek? How does this passage inform our understanding of priests and tithes?

[Read about Melchizedek in Genesis 14:18–20. Discover more in Hebrews 7:1–17.]

10. ELIEZER (1)

By name, this Eliezer only appears once in the Bible. He is from Damascus and a servant of Abram. We can assume that Eliezer is Abram's lead servant and most esteemed, because Abram is childless at the time and identifies Eliezer as the heir of his estate.

If Abram dies childless, Eliezer will inherit much. Therefore, from a financial standpoint, Eliezer has every reason to hope that Abram never has any children.

Yet Abram (Abraham) and Sarah do at last have a son. His name is Isaac. They want to find a wife for him from their own people. And they send their trusted servant back home to seek one.

We don't know the name of this trusted servant,

but it's possible that Abraham tasks his lead servant, Eliezer, with this all-important assignment.

This, of course, is speculation, but it's an interesting consideration.

Regardless, the servant is successful and finds a wife for Isaac. Her name is Rebekah.

How well are we doing at living a trustworthy life? When someone has an all-important assignment, how likely are they to pick us?

[Read about Eliezer in Genesis 15:2–5. Discover more in Genesis 24.]

11. JUDITH (1) AND BASEMATH (1)

Judith and Basemath only show up in one passage in the Bible. They are co-wives of Esau. First Esau marries Judith. She's the daughter of a Hittite man named Beeri. Then Esau marries Basemath. She's the daughter of another Hittite man, Elon.

These marriages are a source of grief to Esau's parents, Isaac and Rebekah, but we don't know why.

One explanation is that their son's wives are Hittite women. The Hittites are descendants of Canaan, whom Esau's ancestor Noah cursed. The Hittites present an ongoing opposition to God's people throughout much of the Old Testament.

Another consideration is that Esau's marriages to these two women may have been acts of rebellion against his parents. Marrying someone out of rebellion is never a wise idea. It will surely be a source of grief.

We should note that Esau's parents send his brother, Jacob, to find a wife from their own clan. Yet they don't do the same thing for Esau. His only solution to find a wife is to marry a local woman, which he does—twice. (He also later marries his cousin Mahalath, perhaps trying to appease his parents.)

A final consideration is that their grief stems from the fact that he married multiple women instead of one. After seeing the misery dual wives caused Isaac's father, Abraham, they may hope to spare their son that turmoil.

Regardless of their reasons, Esau's parents grieved over what he did.

What things may we have done out of rebellion against our parents that caused them to grieve? What things may we have done out of rebellion that caused God to grieve?

[Read about Judith and Basemath in Genesis 26:34–35. Discover more about grief in Proverbs 10:1.]

12. DEBORAH (1)

Rebekah agrees to leave her family to travel to a distant land to marry her cousin Isaac. Her family sends her off, along with her nurse. This suggests Rebekah may be quite young at the time and still in need of adult care.

It's interesting to note that although Rebekah decides to leave her family and travel far away, Rebekah's nurse has no choice in the matter. She'll never see her family and friends again.

We later learn the nurse's name is Deborah, but we know nothing more about her or what she does.

The Bible does, however, record Deborah's death. We don't know why, because she seems like an incidental character in the history of God's

More Old Testament Sinners and Saints

people. Regardless, it must have been important for God to note her passing in Scripture.

Whether our life receives celebration, becomes a mere footnote in history, or fades from memory, what we do is important to God. And that's what matters most.

Do we do things to get the world's attention or is God's opinion what matters most?

[Read about Deborah in Genesis 35:8. Discover more in Genesis 24:59–61.]

13. ER (1)

Jacob's son Judah leaves his family and travels to Adullam. There he marries a Canaanite woman, a descendant of Canaan, which as a group Noah cursed.

They have three sons. The oldest is Er, followed by Onan, and then Shelah.

Judah finds a wife for his firstborn son, Er. Her name is Tamar (1).

All we know about Er is that he is wicked in God's sight, so God kills him.

Does this idea of being wicked in God's sight sound familiar? Back in the days of Noah, God saw the wickedness of all people and destroyed them with a flood.

Though we don't know the details about Er's

More Old Testament Sinners and Saints

wicked behavior, we do know it was severe enough for God to end his life right away. Though we all deserve death for our sins, it's seldom immediate. Er's punishment, however, is swift and final.

Thankfully, Jesus will later provide a solution to the death sentence we all face.

How does knowing that God sees all our sins affect us? Though none of us are as wicked as Er, our sins do separate us from God. Have you turned to Jesus to be reconciled with the Father?

[Read about Er in Genesis 38:6–7. Discover more about wickedness in Genesis 6:5–6.]

14. ONAN

After God kills Er for his extreme wickedness, Er's father, Judah, passes the dead man's widow, Tamar (1), to his second child, Onan. The intent is that Onan will produce children for his deceased brother to carry on his family line through Tamar.

Judah tells Onan it's his responsibility as Tamar's brother-in-law to do this.

Onan complies only in part. Though Onan uses Tamar to satisfy himself, he keeps her from getting pregnant. In doing so, he fails to obey his father and do what's expected of him.

God is not pleased. He views Onan's act as wicked.

Some take this story as confirmation that birth

control displeases God, but the context focuses on Onan's failure to produce a child for his sister-in-law.

Though this expectation is distasteful to us today, it was the custom back then. And Onan fails to fulfill his responsibility.

God views it as wicked and kills Onan right away, just like he did with Onan's brother Er.

When have we not done what our parents told us to do? How does God view our disobedience?

[Read about Onan in Genesis 38:8–10. Discover more in a parallel story in Matthew 22:23–28.]

15. SHELAH (3)

God has killed Shelah's older brothers, Er and Onan, for their extreme wickedness.

The custom of the people is that Er's widow, Tamar (1), should be passed to the third brother so he can produce offspring through her for his dead brother. But Shelah isn't old enough. So Judah sends Tamar home to live with her parents until Shelah grows up, pledging that she will one day marry him.

Yet Judah doesn't follow through on his promise to Tamar. He fears that Shelah will die just like Er and Onan. This suggests that Judah may blame Tamar for his sons' deaths. He doesn't want to risk

More Old Testament Sinners and Saints

the life of his only remaining son, so he withholds Shelah from Tamar.

As a result, Tamar takes extreme action to get what is due to her and what Judah promised to give.

Though Shelah's presence brings about these events, he does nothing good or bad to make them happen.

We know nothing about his character. But we do know that God views his older brothers as wicked and doesn't proclaim the same judgment on Shelah.

This suggests that Shelah isn't like his brothers and chooses a better path.

What negative traits of our family and friends should we avoid? What admirable traits of our family and friends should we follow?

[Read about Shelah in Genesis 38:11–14. Discover another son who stood out from his brothers in 1 Samuel 16:1–13.]

16. PEREZ

After Tamar (1) tricks Judah into impregnating her, she gives birth to twins. They are Perez and Zerah.

The name Perez means "breaking out," because he broke out of the womb first before his twin brother.

Though we know nothing more about Perez and what he did, future generations esteem him. When Boaz marries the widowed and childless Ruth several centuries later, the townspeople proclaim blessings on her. They say, "may your family be like that of Perez, whom Tamar bore to Judah" (Ruth 4:12).

And this blessing comes to be.

Ruth has Obed, who is the father of Jesse and

the grandfather of King David. Matthew's genealogy of Jesus honors all four (Matthew 1:5–6), as with their ancestor Perez (Matthew 1:3).

Though Perez's conception occurred in a duplicitous situation, he made his life matter.

What can we do to make our lives matter? How can we rise above our circumstances and not let them define us?

[Read about Perez in Genesis 38:27–30. Discover more in Luke 3:33.]

17. ZERAH (3)

Zerah is the younger twin of Perez. They are sons of Judah and Tamar (1).

When Tamar is in labor, the hand of one of her babies emerges. The midwife ties a scarlet thread around his wrist. Then the hand withdraws.

The baby who is born first, however, doesn't have the scarlet thread around his wrist. The baby who's born second, does. They name him Zerah, which means "scarlet" or "brightness."

Though Zerah is nearly born first, he isn't. His brother Perez beats him. Birth order is important to the people at that time. As a result, Zerah's parents elevate Perez's life over Zerah's.

Zerah no doubt grew up hearing the story of his

hand emerging first and the midwife tying a scarlet thread around it. But his brother enters the world before him.

We can suspect Zerah spends his life wondering what might have happened had he been born first.

In what areas of our lives do we wonder what might have been? How can we move beyond what we wish had happened in the past to make a difference today?

[Read about Zerah in Genesis 38:27–30. Discover another set of twins in Genesis 25:21–34.]

18. POTIPHAR'S WIFE

Joseph is an attractive man. Potiphar's wife notices. She pursues Joseph.

We don't know her motivation. Does her husband ignore her? Is she bored? Perhaps she's merely promiscuous. Yet her reasons don't matter. She tries to seduce Joseph.

Joseph resists. He explains why he won't sleep with her, but she ignores his words, focusing only on her lust to be with him. This goes on day after day.

Joseph strives to stay away from her or makes sure someone is always around whenever she's nearby. But one day, as he goes about his work, she realizes they are alone. She becomes aggressive. She grabs him and draws him toward her. He pulls away. In his haste to escape her grasp, he leaves his cloak in her hands as he flees.

Unable to satisfy her desires, her lust turns to revenge.

She calls for her servants and spins a lie about what happened, of how Joseph pursued her, of how she screamed for help, and of how he ran off. She holds up his jacket as proof. When Potiphar gets home, she repeats her lies to him. In a rage, he throws Joseph in prison, where he languishes for years.

Potiphar's wife is an immoral woman who makes no effort to control her sexual desires. She is an unfaithful spouse—or at least she tries to be one. When she can't seduce Joseph or convince him to sleep with her, she concocts lies to destroy him.

How far will we go to get what we want, even when it's wrong? How low will we stoop to hurt those who get in our way?

[Read about Potiphar's wife in Genesis 39:1–20. Discover a different encounter in 2 Samuel 13:1–19.]

19. POTIPHAR

Through a series of events outside his control, Joseph has become a slave owned by Potiphar. Potiphar is one of Pharaoh's officials and captain of the guard.

God's favor is on Joseph in Potiphar's household, and he proves himself to the captain. Potiphar eventually puts his entire estate under the care of his slave. Potiphar's home and property prosper because of Joseph's diligent work and God's blessing on him.

Joseph conducts himself so well that Potiphar trusts him with everything. His only concern at home is what he will eat. Joseph handles all else.

But one day this perfect situation falls apart.

Potiphar's wife comes to him in a rage, claiming that Joseph tried to rape her.

Furious, Potiphar throws Joseph into prison.

Though we may assume Potiphar does this because of what he believes Joseph did, why didn't he take a harsher action? As captain of the guard, we can assume he has the power to do something more punitive than prison. And since Joseph is a slave, he has no rights. Could Potiphar have used his power to execute Joseph?

But what if prison is an act of mercy, something done out of esteem for Joseph? Perhaps Potiphar suspects his wife is to blame and not his servant. Has she cheated on him in the past? What if Potiphar knows in his spirit that Joseph is innocent, that he's the victim?

If this is the case, Potiphar can't punish his wife without the situation becoming public. And if he dismisses her allegations by doing nothing, that would only strain his relationship with his wife even more. In this instance, we see that throwing Joseph in prison is the easiest recourse for Potiphar.

Regardless of the reasons behind Potiphar's actions, the fact remains that innocent Joseph lands in prison.

When we hear a condemning story about someone, do we believe it or try to verify the truth? How can we rectify our mistake when we believe what someone told us, only to later learn it was a lie?

[Read about Potiphar in Genesis 39:1–20. Discover what happens to Joseph next in Genesis 40.]

20. ASENATH

Pharaoh later gives the-now-freed Joseph a wife. Her name is Asenath, and she's the daughter of the priest of On. The priest's name is Potiphera. (Don't confuse Potiphera with Potiphar.) This is likely a strategic move on Pharaoh's part, hoping that Asenath will influence Joseph to accept Egyptian perspectives and beliefs.

In this way, Pharaoh uses Asenath to accomplish his goal. He expects her to influence her husband for her country. But she has no say in his plan.

We know Joseph is both attractive and powerful, but he's also an outsider. He isn't even permitted to eat at the same table as the Egyptians. Asenath is forced to marry a foreigner. There is no hint of love or affection between the two. Though this could be a good life for her, it's doubtful it's the one she wanted.

Asenath and Joseph have two sons, Manasseh and Ephraim, but we know nothing else of the couple's relationship. We don't know if Joseph influences his wife to believe in God, but in looking at the life of Joseph, we see no hint that Asenath causes him to embrace her people's way of life or turn from God.

When others try to use us, do we become their pawn or make our own path? How should we react if we're in a marriage we don't want?

[Read about Asenath in Genesis 41:45–50. Discover a man whose foreign wives influenced him in 1 Kings 11:1–13.]

21. MANASSEH AND EPHRAIM

Joseph and Asenath have two sons. The oldest is Manasseh, and the younger is Ephraim. They are the grandsons of Jacob, later called Israel.

When Israel is on his deathbed, Joseph comes to see his ailing father, bringing his two sons, Manasseh and Ephraim, with him. Hearing about Joseph's arrival, Israel rallies and sits up in bed.

He makes a curious statement to his son. Israel elevates his two grandsons, Manasseh and Ephraim, and mentions them along with his own sons. In this way, Israel grants these two boys the same status as their uncles. All will receive their inheritance through Israel. This, in effect, gives Joseph's descendants a double portion, something due to the firstborn son.

Though Joseph is not Israel's firstborn, he is Rachel's. Since the now-deceased Rachel was Israel's favorite wife, we can understand him seeking to give Joseph a double portion through his boys.

Israel first blesses Joseph. Next, he blesses Manasseh and Ephraim. Israel, however, blesses Ephraim as the older son and Manasseh as the younger.

When Joseph tries to correct his father's error, Israel confirms it is not a mistake. He declares that the younger Ephraim will be greater than the older Manasseh.

Yet we don't see much in Scripture to indicate that Ephraim does in fact become greater than Manasseh.

Four centuries later, when Israel's numerous descendants leave Egypt, Moses notes that Ephraim's tribe numbers 40,500, with Manasseh's tribe about 20 percent less at 32,200. Yet forty years later when they leave the desert, things are the opposite. Manasseh's descendants have increased to 52,700, while the number of Ephraim's descendants have shrunk to 32,500.

We should keep in mind that during these forty years in the desert, all who entered it died there (except for Joshua and Caleb). It is their offspring that the second census counts. Therefore, Manasseh's tribe flourished in the desert and Ephraim's did not.

When they reach the promised land, Manasseh's descendants divide into two groups, with half receiving an inheritance east of the Jordan and the rest, west of the Jordan. Each group becomes a half tribe of Manasseh.

If anything, it seems that Manasseh becomes greater than Ephraim, despite Israel's blessing.

Do we let our birth order define us? When someone proclaims a blessing over us, how much confidence do we place in their words?

[Read about Manasseh and Ephraim in Genesis 48:1–20. Discover more in Numbers 1:32–35 and Numbers 26:34–37.]

22. SHIPHRAH AND PUAH (2)

Shiphrah and Puah are two Hebrew midwives. They live toward the end of the Israelites' enslavement in Egypt.

The Pharaoh of Egypt, fearing their slaves' mounting numbers, tells Shiphrah and Puah to kill all the baby Israelite boys as they are being born. This is worse than, in effect, performing abortions. It is euthanasia.

But Shiphrah and Puah fear God more than Egypt's pharaoh. So they disregard the king's order and continue to attend to the birth of the Israelite boys, doing everything they can to ensure their survival.

When the Pharaoh confronts them for not doing as he commanded, the two midwives lie.

More Old Testament Sinners and Saints

They tell him they don't arrive in time to do anything. Pharaoh accepts their excuse.

Though they did lie to the Pharaoh, God honors them for their integrity and protecting the Israelite baby boys. He rewards them, giving them their own families.

Sometimes doing the right thing means disobeying human authority and manmade laws. God may honor us as a result, but we could also suffer consequences for our actions.

We should strive to do what God wants us to, regardless of the risk or the outcome.

How willing are we to do what is right? Is lying to protect ourselves ever a justifiable action?

[Read about Shiphrah and Puah in Exodus 1:15–21. Discover more about another woman who lied in Genesis 31:33–35.]

23. REUEL (2)/JETHRO

When Moses flees Egypt for his life, he ends up in the desert. There he encounters the seven daughters of Reuel, a Midianite priest. The girls are shepherdesses. When they try to draw water from the well for their sheep, however, other shepherds drive them away. Moses intervenes for them and waters their flock.

Reuel (later called Jethro) is grateful, and he invites Moses to stay with them. He gives his daughter Zipporah to Moses in marriage.

The next time we encounter Reuel in the Bible is several years later. This is after Moses leads his people out of Egypt. The Bible now calls him

More Old Testament Sinners and Saints

Jethro. We don't know why Reuel changed his name, but he did.

Jethro goes to the desert to meet Moses, returning Moses's wife and sons to him. Moses tells Jethro all that God has done, and Jethro praises the Almighty.

The next day he watches as Moses takes a seat to judge the people as they gather to receive his ruling on their cases. This takes all day. Jethro realizes this is too much for Moses to handle on his own. He advises his son-in-law to train capable men to hear the easier cases. Only the most complicated ones will need Moses's attention. This will lighten Moses's load of leading the people.

Moses follows his father-in-law's wise advice.

How open are we to follow the recommendations of others? Should we give advice to people who haven't asked for it?

[Read about Reuel in Exodus 2:16–21. Read about Jethro in Exodus 18. Discover more in Exodus 4:18.]

24. ZIPPORAH

When Moses flees for his life, he meets seven shepherdesses, the daughters of Reuel. Moses marries one of the daughters, Zipporah. Moses and Zipporah have two sons. They are Gershom and Eliezer.

Years later when Moses and his family travel to Egypt, God afflicts Moses. This is apparently because Moses failed to circumcise his son Gershom, as God commanded the Israelites to do through Abraham.

Just as God is about to kill Moses for his disobedience, Zipporah acts. She pulls out a knife and circumcises Gershom. She touches Moses with the removed foreskin. This appeases God, and he spares Moses.

Zipporah does what her husband did not do. She obeys God's command and saves her husband's life.

How willing are we to act when others fail to? How can we discern when to intervene and when not to?

[Read about Zipporah in Exodus 2:21–22 and Exodus 4:24–26. Discover more in Exodus 18:2–6.]

25. GERSHOM (1) AND ELIEZER (2)

Moses and Zipporah have two sons, Gershom and Eliezer.

The oldest is Gershom. His name means *a foreigner there* because Moses says he's a foreigner in a foreign land.

The younger son is Eliezer. His name means *God is my helper*. Moses acknowledges God as the helper who saved him from Pharaoh's attempt to kill him.

When we consider Moses's close relationship with God and how he successfully leads God's people from Egypt to the promised land, we expect to see this carry over to Moses's boys. Yet the Bible doesn't say this happens.

Instead, Gershom and Eliezer lead unremarkable lives. Scripture doesn't show them as walking closely with the Almighty like their father. Nor does it portray them in any sort of leadership capacity.

Moses could have modeled his deep relationship with God for Gershom and Eliezer to emulate. But there's no indication he did, contrary to the command God gave the people through Moses (Deuteronomy 6:6–9).

Moses could have trained his boys to follow him in leadership, but he did not. It's Moses's protégé, Joshua, who takes over for the exceptional leader and not Moses's sons.

Gershom and Eliezer accomplish nothing noteworthy.

What must we do to pass our faith on to our family and those under our influence? If we come from a strong legacy, what are we doing to continue it?

[Read about Gershom and Eliezer in Exodus 18:2–4. Discover more in 1 Chronicles 23:15–17.]

26. JANNES AND JAMBRES

It may surprise you to see Jannes and Jambres in our discussion of Old Testament sinners and saints. This is because they don't appear in the Old Testament. They show up in the New Testament and then only once. Yet the reference ties them to Moses, so this places them in the Old Testament timeline.

Paul, in writing to his protégé Timothy, talks about how people will act in the last days. (It's a description that seems most apt to our world today.)

Paul warns Timothy to have nothing to do with such people. The teacher goes on to explain why. These people oppose truth, just as Jannes and Jambres opposed Moses.

We can surmise that the story of Jannes and Jambres is part of the Hebrew oral tradition passed down from one generation to the next, which Timothy would have heard from his grandmother Lois and mother Eunice. But we're left to speculate what this opposition might have been. With Moses facing much resistance as the leader of God's chosen people, we have many scenarios to choose from.

Though we don't know the specifics, we can be sure that Timothy does. Paul equates the opposition that Timothy will face with the opposition that Moses faced.

We are safe to assume that Moses prevailed against his foes. In this way, Timothy receives encouragement to prevail in his situation against those who will oppose him. Surely this heartens the young leader.

Who can we encourage on their faith journey? What from our family's oral tradition should we teach to encourage future generations?

[Read about Jannes and Jambres in 2 Timothy 3:8. Discover more about opposition in Exodus 23:20–22.]

27. NADAB (1) AND ABIHU

Aaron has four sons. They are Nadab, Abihu, Eleazar, and Ithamar. With Aaron as the first priest, all four boys are destined to follow him. With Nadab and Abihu as the oldest two, they take the lead in this.

Nadab and Abihu, however, fail to follow God's precise guidelines of worship. Whether it's sloppiness or arrogance, we don't know, but they offer fire and incense to God, contrary to his command. Scripture calls it "unauthorized fire."

As a result of their disobedience, God sends fire to kill them. God's punishment is swift and final.

The Almighty doesn't offer them mercy for their disobedience, just judgment. But fortunately for us today, through Jesus, we can receive the Lord's mercy.

What would we change in our lives if God punished us immediately? When have we relied on God's mercy and grace when we should have stopped doing something wrong?

[Read about Nadab and Abihu in Leviticus 10:1–3, as well as Numbers 26:60–61. Discover more in Numbers 3:1–4.]

28. ELEAZAR (1) AND ITHAMAR

God strikes down Nadab and Abihu for their disobedience. Without any heirs, this means that all the priestly duties now fall to their brothers, Eleazar and Ithamar.

Though all four brothers should have served God together, the work now goes to the two remaining sons of Aaron. As a result, they have twice as much work to do.

As they serve God, we can suspect they do so with much care, remembering the immediate deaths of their brothers for not diligently following God's detailed instructions. They've seen firsthand what could happen if they disobey. This surely guides them and their work for the rest of their lives.

Though we see nothing in Scripture to confirm the work they do, we also don't see anything to criticize it. We can, therefore, assume that God affirms their work as his priests.

There is one incident, however, where things could have gone awry. Right after their older brothers die, Uncle Moses gives Eleazar and Ithamar some instructions on making offerings. They don't do everything Moses expected, and he's angry. Their father, Aaron, however, intervenes on their behalf, and Moses takes no action against them.

God's silence in this matter suggests he's not concerned about what these two priests did.

When have we criticized someone when God may not have cared? How can we discern between knowing when to stand up for God and when to be silent?

[Read about Eleazar and Ithamar in Leviticus 10:6–20. Discover more in Numbers 3:4.]

29. KORAH (3)

Korah is the son of Izhar, the son of Kohath, the son of Levi. He leads a rebellion against Aaron, Moses . . . and God.

The descendants of Levi are set apart from the rest of the Israelites for a special role. They are to work in the tabernacle and assist the priests in ministering to the people. But this isn't enough for Korah. He wants to be a priest too.

He brings with him three men from the tribe of Reuben. They are Dathan, Abiram, and On. And they rally 250 men to join them. They all want to serve as priests and don't feel this role is only for descendants of Aaron.

Though they may be doing this to elevate themselves into a more prominent position, they could also have pure motives, wanting to serve God more fully. Yet this doesn't make it right.

Korah challenges Moses. Distraught, Moses proposes a spiritual showdown.

The next day, Korah and his followers are to each take a censer with fire and incense to present to the Lord. Aaron will do the same. Then God will pick who he wants.

The actions and attitudes of Korah and his followers displease God. He reacts immediately. The ground opens and swallows Korah, Dathan, and Abiram, their families, and their possessions. Then God sends fire from heaven to consume the 250 men offering incense.

God makes it clear he wants only Aaron (and later his descendants) to serve him as priest.

When have our spiritual aspirations not pleased God? How can we discern when to strive for more and when to be content with the position God has given us?

[Read about Korah in Numbers 16. Discover more in Exodus 6:18–24.]

30. PHINEHAS (1)

Phinehas is the son of Eleazar, the son of Aaron. This means that Phinehas is Aaron's grandson.

While the Israelites are in the desert getting ready to take the promised land, an issue of sexual immorality arises between some of the men and Moabite women. This effectively aligns them with Baal. The Lord is infuriated and orders their execution.

Even as the people mourn the death of these men, one Israelite man doesn't understand—or doesn't care. He brings a Midianite woman into camp and into his tent. Everyone sees this. It's as if he's flaunting what he's going to do.

Phinehas won't have it. He grabs a spear. Going

into the man's tent, he drives it through the man and into the woman. God's anger subsides. A plague that has already killed 24,000 people stops.

Though we may question Phinehas for his judgment and violent action, God does not. He implicitly affirms it.

But it's an overstretch to interpret this passage as advocating violence—even murder—in God's name. A better conclusion is to be ready to take decisive action for the things that matter to God.

Phinehas acted with zeal, and this pleased God.

In what is a likely connection, Phinehas emerges as the leading priest among his generation.

When have we been passive when we should have acted? When have we overreacted when a more God-honoring approach would have been moderation?

[Read about Phinehas in Numbers 25:6–13. Discover more in Numbers 31:6–7 and Joshua 22:13–33.]

31. KOZBI

The nation of Israel has a problem with sexual immorality. Some of their men are involved with Moabite women, indulging themselves sexually with these foreigners, something the law of Moses prohibits. Then these women entice the men to worship with them and offer sacrifices to Baal instead of God.

God is not pleased. Moses orders the execution of each man who has strayed.

During all this, another man brings a Midianite woman into camp and into his tent. Her name is Kozbi. We don't know if he thinks this is okay because she is a Midianite and not a Moabite. Perhaps he wants to make a point or maybe he isn't thinking at all. We also don't know if Kozbi is aware of the situation. What we do know is that this man flaunts his sexual relationship with a foreign woman, a liaison God forbids and for which many other men have just died.

Phinehas, the priest, takes judgment into his hands in the form of a spear. Going into the tent, he drives the shaft all the way through the man and into Kozbi. This appeases God's wrath.

While Kozbi may have instigated this, it's more likely she is merely a naïve woman who ends up in the wrong place. But she pays for her ignorance with her life.

Being unaware is no excuse for doing wrong. There will still be consequences for our actions.

What must we do to guard ourselves from sexual immorality? If we intentionally sin, do we rely on God's mercy or fear his judgment?

[Read about Kozbi in Numbers 25:6–18. Discover more in Numbers 25:1–5.]

32. ZELOPHEHAD

Zelophehad has five daughters but no sons. His girls are Mahlah, Noah (2), Hoglah, Milkah (2), and Tirzah. Zelophehad dies in the desert before he can receive his allotment of property in the promised land. Since he has no sons to receive his inheritance in his stead, the girls will get nothing.

They boldly go before Moses and ask for their father's share, contrary to convention. God tells Moses to include them in the land assignments, which Joshua later carries out.

With a population of millions, there are surely other women in this same situation. But only Zelophehad's daughters come forward.

In this way, Zelophehad's descendants receive property in the promised land.

Are we willing to speak up to receive what is due us? Will we trust God with the outcome?

[Read about Zelophehad in Numbers 27:1–7. Discover more in Numbers 36:1–12 and Joshua 17:3–6.]

33. ACHAN

At last it's time for Joshua to lead the people into the land God promised to give them and take it. First up is Jericho. But they don't attack the city as we'd expect. Instead, they march around it for seven days.

On the seventh day, the priests blow their trumpets, the people shout, and the walls fall. They burn the entire city and everything in it but keep the gold and silver, putting it into the treasury, just as God commanded. Only Rahab and her family survive (Joshua 6:17–25).

Next up is Ai. It's a small town with few inhabitants. The spies recommend that an army of two or three thousand can easily take the city. But Ai routs them and kills three dozen men.

Distraught, Joshua seeks God. That's when God shares that someone failed to follow his exacting instructions when taking Jericho.

When God reveals that the guilty person is Achan, he admits his sin in taking a beautiful robe, silver, and gold from the city and hiding them in his tent.

Though he confesses his sin, he doesn't receive forgiveness. Instead, he receives judgment. The people stone him to death, along with his family and possessions. Then they burn everything.

With God's wrath now appeased, the people attack the city of Ai. This time they do exactly what God says. This time they're victorious (Joshua 8:1–29).

How well do we do at obeying God's commands? When have we last thanked Jesus for forgiving our sins?

[Read about Achan in Joshua 7. Discover another person who failed to obey God's command to utterly destroy a city in 1 Samuel 15:1–31.]

34. EHUD (1)

It takes some time for God's people to take possession of the land he promised them. Once they do, a distressing cycle recurs. They turn from God and do evil, he allows a foreign power to conquer them, and they cry out to the Lord for help. In response he sends them a judge—a military leader—to free them.

Such is the case with Ehud.

Because of the Israelites' disobedience to God, he allows the king of Moab to subject them to his control for eighteen years. When they cry out for help, he sends Ehud.

This story has two interesting elements. First, Ehud is left-handed. Second, the king of Moab is extremely overweight. Here's what happens.

Ehud leads the delegation to pay their annual tribute to Moab. After they complete their mission and leave, Ehud heads back. He tells the king he has a secret message to share.

The guards likely assumed Ehud is right-handed and looked for a weapon on his left as would be the norm, but not the other side. Therefore, Ehud's sword escapes detection.

The king sends everyone away. We can envision Ehud extending his right hand in a friendly gesture as he approaches the king to deliver the message. With the king distracted and feeling safe, Ehud stealthily draws his sword with his left hand and thrusts it into the King's belly. The 18-inch sword (close to half a meter) plunges into the king's belly and his fat covers the hilt.

Ehud locks the doors and flees through the terrace. He escapes before anyone realizes the king is dead.

Ehud summons the army, and they attack Moab, killing ten thousand of their troops. With this victory over their enemy, Moab is now subject to Israel. And the people live in peace for eighty years.

What bold action may God be calling us to make? Seeing how one person can make a difference, what can we do today?

[Read about Ehud in Judges 3:12–30. Discover a similar story in 2 Samuel 3:22–30.]

35. ABIMELEK (2)

Abimelek is the son of Gideon (also called Jerub-Baal). The Bible first lists Abimelek's mother as Gideon's concubine and later as his slave. Either way, the boy has a less-than-ideal start to life. But this does not excuse his behavior as an adult. He could have risen above the circumstances of his birth. But, as we will soon see, he does not.

Abimelek has seventy half-brothers. Yes, seventy. This means Gideon fathered children with many women. Abimelek goes to Shechem, where his mother is from, and asks if they want him to rule them—as one of their own—or if they want Gideon's seventy sons. The people choose him and give him money.

More Old Testament Sinners and Saints

Abimelek uses the funds to raise an army of "reckless scoundrels." He returns home to Ophrah, where he murders his half-brothers. Only the youngest, Jotham (1), escapes.

The people of Shechem make Abimelek their king.

After three years, God causes a rift between Abimelek and the people. He does this to bring about the punishment of Abimelek for murdering his brothers—and the people of Shechem for their indirect role.

A man named Gaal moves to Shechem. He opposes Abimelek. The two go into battle, with Gaal leading the people of Shechem against Abimelek and his hired army. Abimelek prevails. The next day, he takes revenge on the town of Shechem. He kills all the people. Since all his mother's relatives live there, he presumably kills them too. He destroys the city.

Then Abimelek attacks the city of Thebez. He besieges it and captures it. Inside the city, the people flee to a tower. As Abimelek approaches the stronghold to burn it and the people inside, a woman drops an upper millstone. It hits Abimelek and cracks his skull.

Lest it be said a woman killed him, Abimelek

instructs his armor-bearer to run him through. The servant does.

Abimelek dies having done nothing positive in his life. He leaves a legacy of evil, having caused the death of many—and himself.

How can we rise above our past to make a better future for ourselves and others? What sort of legacy are we leaving?

[Read about Abimelek in Judges 9. Discover more about Shechem in Genesis 34.]

36. JOTHAM (1)

When Abimelek returns home to murder his seventy brothers, only Jotham, the youngest one, survives. He hides to escape execution.

When Jotham learns the people of Shechem have made his half-brother their king, he climbs a mountain. From this lofty position, he shouts to them.

He shares a story about trees looking for a king to rule over them. Each one they ask, declines. At last, the thornbush agrees.

In doing so, he implies that Abimelek is the thornbush, as well as the least desirable choice as Shechem's ruler.

Then Jotham criticizes their foolishness in

making Abimelek king instead of letting his brothers continue their father Gideon's legacy.

To conclude, Jotham proclaims curses on Abimelek for the murder of his brothers and on Shechem for helping.

Then he flees and hides in fear. This is the last we hear of Jotham.

Scripture concludes the pathetic tale of Abimelek's life noting this was how God punished the evil man for killing his brothers, as well as destroying the wicked city of Shechem for facilitating it.

This fulfills Jotham's curse.

What do we think about Jotham pronouncing a curse on Abimelek? What is an area where we should proclaim truth like Jotham?

[Read about Jotham in Judges 9:5–21. Discover more in Judges 9:56–57.]

37. GAAL

We know nothing about Gaal except what appears in this passage in the book of Judges. Though the text often mentions him as the son of Ebed, Scripture tells us nothing about his father either.

What we do know is that Gaal moves with his family to the town of Shechem. This is during the time of Abimelek's rule. Gaal earns the town's respect, and they put their trust in him. During the grape harvest, they hold a festival, eating and drinking in celebration. It's then that the people—perhaps inebriated—curse Abimelek.

Gaal builds on their dissatisfaction and questions Abimelek's fitness to rule. "If only I had an army," Gaal muses, "I would get rid of him."

The townspeople rally behind Gaal's leadership and go out with him to fight.

But Zebul, the governor of Shechem, warns Abimelek of Gaal's coup attempt. Abimelek is ready and defeats Gaal's army, killing many.

Zebul drives Gaal and his family out of Shechem. The troublemaker is gone.

When have we gone some place new and tried to change it? What was the outcome?

[Read about Gaal in Judges 9:26–41. Discover a comparable situation in 2 Samuel 15:1–4.]

38. JEPHTHAH

Jephthah is the son of Gilead and a prostitute. Gilead and his wife have other sons, who drive Jephthah away, lest they must share their inheritance with him. Jephthah forms a gang of troublemakers.

Some time later, the Ammonites fight Israel. In desperation, the elders of Gilead ask Jephthah to lead them into battle. He agrees, but then makes a rash vow.

Jephthah pledges that upon his successful return he will sacrifice the first thing that comes through the door of his house as a burnt offering to thank God for his victory. Jephthah assumes it will be an animal.

He is indeed victorious.

To his dismay, the first thing that walks through the door when he returns home is his daughter. She dances in celebration for his success. She is his only child. He laments the foolish promise he made to God but feels obligated to fulfill it.

We don't know the name of Jephthah's daughter, but we do grieve her fate. She doesn't complain about her father's careless promise. Instead, she confirms he must follow through. Her only request is a two-month reprieve to mourn her misfortune with her friends. We applaud her steadfast confidence in how she accepts her father's pledge, revealing her deep faith in God.

Then Jephthah follows through on his vow.

What's unclear is if Jephthah physically sacrifices his daughter, something Moses prohibited, or if her life is redeemed for service to God, like Hannah will later do in giving her son Samuel to serve God in the temple.

Regardless, it's clear that Jephthah's daughter will not enjoy the future she expected, for she willingly accepts the consequences of her father's impulsive vow to God. We commend her for her pious attitude, all the while being reminded to be careful with what we promise.

When have we made a rash vow? Whether we followed through or reneged, what do we feel about our response to our unwise promise?

[Read about Jephthah in Judges 11. Discover more in the story of Hannah and Samuel in 1 Samuel 1:10–22.]

39. MICAH (1)

Though Micah appears in the book of Judges, we'd be wrong to consider him a judge. He never judged or led the people. In fact, the Bible doesn't record a single good thing he does. Here's an overview:

Micah steals eleven hundred shekels of silver from his mother. Not knowing who the robber is, she curses the person who took her money.

When Micah reveals himself as the thief, she in turn blesses him. She consecrates the silver to the Lord and commissions a silversmith to make an idol. This is precisely what she shouldn't do with silver she dedicated to God, but she does.

Micah puts the idol in a shrine he had made.

The shrine also contains an ephod and other idols. One of his sons serves as priest.

When a Levite from Bethlehem happens by, Micah installs him as priest and provides for him. Never mind that a Levite isn't supposed to serve as a priest, especially not at a shrine of idols. But this Levite doesn't care. He just wants a place to stay and to do something he feels is important.

Some spies from the tribe of Dan stop by. They're on a mission. They inquire of the priest about their journey. He gives them God's approval and sends them away in peace.

Later the spies return with an army, intent on conquering a nearby city. They take Micah's idol, his ephod, and his household gods. They talk Micah's priest into going with them. Micah chases them but later gives up when he realizes he'll lose.

The army from Dan conquers the city and burns it. Then they rebuild it and settle there. They worship the idol Micah made.

Everything in the story of Micah is contrary to the laws of Moses and disrespects the Lord. This is Micah's legacy.

What conclusions can we draw from Micah's mom proclaiming both a curse and a blessing? What have we consecrated or dedicated to the Lord?

[Read about Micah in Judges 17–18. Discover another dedication in Judges 16:17.]

40. MAHLON AND KILION

Mahlon and Kilion are the sons of Elimelek and Naomi. During the time of the judges, there's a famine. In search of food, the family moves from Bethlehem to Moab and settles there.

Elimelek dies in Moab. Mahlon and Kilion marry local Moabite girls. Mahlon marries Ruth, and Kilion marries Orpah.

Both Mahlon and Kilion die in Moab too. As a result, all three women are widows—and destitute.

Naomi and Ruth head back to Bethlehem, while Orpah stays in Moab.

It's in Bethlehem that Boaz marries Ruth, who becomes the great-grandmother of King David and ancestor of Jesus.

Had Mahlon and Kilion not died, Naomi and Ruth would have stayed in Moab and Boaz would have never met and married Ruth. It may, however, be an overstretch to say that God caused Mahlon and Kilion's death to accomplish his will.

God, however, does work all things together for good to those who love him and are called to his purpose (Romans 8:28). With this in mind, we can see how the Almighty uses this situation to unite Ruth with Boaz, which otherwise would not have happened.

When a loved one dies, do we blame God? When have we seen our Lord work things out for good in our lives?

[Read about Mahlon and Kilion in Ruth 1:1–5. Discover more in Ruth 4:9–10.]

41. OBED (1)

Obed is Boaz and Ruth's first son. Though Ruth was first married to Mahlon, they had no children. The Bible doesn't mention Boaz and Ruth having any more children, so Obed may be an only child.

The women in the village praise God for Obed's birth. They bless him and proclaim that he will become famous throughout the land. Though we don't know if Obed himself becomes famous, we do know that his grandson—King David—becomes well known and a man after God's own heart (1 Samuel 13:14 and Acts 13:22). David indeed becomes famous.

And Jesus descends from Obed many centuries later. Jesus is even more famous.

What are we known for? What can we do to prepare our children to do amazing things for God?

[Read about Obed in Ruth 4:13–22. Discover more in Matthew 1:5.]

42. JABEZ

Though an entire book was later written about his brief prayer, we know little about Jabez from Scripture. The Bible only mentions him in two obscure verses, buried in a lengthy genealogy.

We know his birth is difficult, and the name his mother gives him reflects the physical pain his arrival caused.

We also know that Jabez is an honorable man, more honorable than others. And he has a deep connection with God, for when he prays a bold prayer, God answers it.

What is his prayer? It has five components:

1. Bless me (so that I may be a blessing to others).

2. Enlarge my territory (which increases my influence).

3. May your hand guide me (for I'd be foolish to try anything on my own).

4. Keep me from harm (that is, keep me safe).

5. Spare me from pain (that is, save me from suffering).

After Jabez makes his bold request, God says, "Yes!"

How well do we do at praying bold prayers? What do we think about adapting Jabez's prayer as our own?

[Read about Jabez in 1 Chronicles 4:9–10. Discover another answered prayer in Judges 16:28–30.]

43. ELKANAH (4)

Elkanah, from the tribe of Ephriam, has two wives. They are Hannah and Peninnah. Having two wives is never a smart idea. Conflict is sure to result. Such is the case between Elkanah's two wives.

The text says Elkanah loves Hannah. The implication is that he does not love Peninnah. Or at least he does not love her as much. This escalates the tension between the two women.

Peninnah has many children, but Hannah has none. Peninnah torments the childless Hannah. Though Elkanah is aware of how Peninnah treats Hannah, he does nothing to protect her or stop the harassment.

His attitude is that he should be more important

to her than even ten sons. In saying this he shows how highly he thinks of himself and how little he thinks of Hannah's longing to have a son.

If we're married, how well do we understand our spouse's feelings and desires? When we see one person treating another unfairly, do we ignore the situation or intervene?

[Read about Elkanah in 1 Samuel 1:1–8. Discover more in 1 Samuel 1:21–23.]

44. HANNAH

Hannah, married to Elkanah, longs to have a son but is childless. Adding to her misery, everyone harasses her. Though she's her husband's favorite wife, he dismisses her infertility. He fails to protect her from the verbal assaults of his other wife, Peninnah, who torments her.

When Hannah prays earnestly, Eli, the priest, accuses her of being drunk. But she's in deep despair over her childless condition and challenging home life.

Hannah cries out to God in anguish, begging him to give her a son. She asks for a boy, not just a child. If God will answer her request, she promises to give the boy to God for a lifetime of service.

God understands Hannah, even though Elkanah, Peninnah, and Eli fail her. The Lord hears her plea and gives her a son.

Hannah names the boy Samuel, saying, "because I asked the Lord for him."

After weaning Samuel, Hannah gives him to Eli for a lifetime of service to God at the temple, just as she promised. When Hannah and her family make their pilgrimage to the temple to offer their sacrifices to God each year, she sees young Samuel and gives him a new robe.

God blesses Hannah with five more children.

As with Hannah, God understands our situation, even when no one else does.

Will we trust God to rescue us from our turmoil? When we make a promise to the Lord, do we follow through and do as we say?

[Read about Hannah in 1 Samuel 1:1–28 and 1 Samuel 2:19–21. Discover more in 1 Samuel 2:1–11.]

45. PENINNAH

Peninnah is a co-wife with Hannah. They're both married to Elkanah.

Reminiscent of Jacob and his two wives, Rachel and Leah, we have the story of Elkanah and his two wives, Hannah and Peninnah. Just as Jacob loves Rachel more than Leah, Elkanah loves Hannah more than Peninnah. Likewise, as Rachel, the favored wife, is childless, so, too, is Hannah.

Another parallel biblical account is of Abraham, Sarah, and Hagar, where Hagar, the wife with a child, harasses Sarah, the wife without one. So too, Peninnah harasses Hannah.

Despite Peninnah producing children for Elkanah, he loves Hannah. Peninnah lashes out by verbally harassing Hannah. Though we shouldn't condone what Peninnah does, we can understand her actions. But that doesn't make what she does right.

When we're in a trying situation, do we seek to make the best of it or harass others? When have we risen above an unfair situation in a God-honoring way?

[Read about Peninnah in 1 Samuel 1:1–6. Discover parallel situations in Genesis 16:1–16 and Genesis 29:14–35.]

46. HOPHNI AND PHINEHAS (2)

Hophni and Phinehas are priests, just like their father Eli. Hophni and Phinehas, however, do not behave as proper priests should.

When the people come to offer their sacrifices, Hophni and Phinehas fail to respect the offerings or handle them as prescribed by Moses. In doing so they show contempt for the gifts the people make to God. Furthermore, Hophni and Phinehas sleep with the women who serve at the tent of meeting.

Eli hears about what his sons are doing and confronts them, trying to get them to change their evil behavior. But his sons don't listen to their father's attempt to correct their actions. They continue doing what they've always done.

One of the Lord's prophets comes to Eli with a harsh rebuke from God. Because of their wickedness, the prophet foretells that Hophni and Phinehas will both die on the same day. In their place, God will provide a new priest, a faithful leader.

Though we may think this new priest alludes to the young boy Samuel, Samuel never becomes a priest (though he does become a great prophet). Samuel can't become a priest because he's not a descendant of Aaron. Instead, this prophecy looks forward to the priesthood of Jesus, anointed to minister forever.

As prophesied, Hophni and Phinehas both die on the same day. In doing so, God ends their wickedness.

How do we respond when God convicts us of our wrong actions? Do we think that, because of God's mercy, we can ignore what he tells us to do?

[Read about Hophni and Phinehas in 1 Samuel 2:12–36. Discover more in 1 Samuel 4:2–11.]

47. ELI

Eli is a priest. He serves the Lord for forty years. When Eli grows older, his two boys, Hophni and Phinehas, take over the daily priestly duties for him, as prescribed by Moses.

While we can assume Eli is a good priest, his boys are not. Scripture says so. When Eli tries to correct his sons' improper behavior as priests, they dismiss his warning.

Though they are adults and responsible for their own actions, the disrespect they show for their father suggests he may have failed to raise them right. Regardless, they surely don't respect what Eli tells them, just as they don't respect God's commands for how they should conduct themselves as priests.

A prophet comes to Eli prophesying that, because of their wickedness, Hophni and Phinehas will die on the same day.

Not only do they die as foretold, but the Philistines also capture the ark of God. When Eli hears the news, he falls backward in his chair, breaks his neck, and dies.

How do the actions of our children (or those under our authority) reflect on us? Will God judge us accordingly if we don't lead our family (or our charges) well?

[Read about Eli in 1 Samuel 2:22–25 and 1 Samuel 4:12–18. Discover more in 1 Kings 2:27.]

48. JESSE

In most of the instances when Jesse appears in Scripture, it's in relation to his son David, as in "David, son of Jesse," or simply "the son of Jesse."

Yet the first time we encounter Jesse in the Bible, this is not the case. Here's what happens:

God has rejected Saul as king and tasks Samuel to appoint a new one. The Lord directs Samuel to go to Jesse in the town of Bethlehem. There Samuel is to anoint one of Jesse's sons as king. God doesn't tell Samuel which boy to pick, merely that he'll indicate which one when the time comes.

When Samuel sees Jesse's oldest son, Eliab, the prophet assumes he is the one God wants. But he is not. Neither is Jesse's second son, Abinadab, nor the third son, Shammah.

Jesse presents all seven of his boys to Samuel, but God doesn't pick any of them. When Samuel presses Jesse, he admits he has one more son, David, who's out tending the sheep. It's as if Jesse forgot David. Surely, he dismissed his youngest son as not being worthy.

But God sees things differently than Jesse and differently than we do. He directs Samuel to anoint David as king. The least of Jesse's sons will become the greatest.

When have we dismissed any of our family or friends, failing to see them as God sees them? When has God surprised us by who he picked to serve him?

[Read about Jesse in 1 Samuel 16:1–13. Discover more in 1 Samuel 17:12–18.]

49. GOLIATH

Even though Scripture contains only one story about Goliath, most people know it well. This, however, is not for his valor but for his arrogance.

Goliath serves in the Philistine army. He stands out because he's taller than everyone else. His stature is an amazing nine feet.

The Israelite army squares off against the Philistine army, with a valley separating them. Each morning Goliath comes out and taunts them. He challenges them to send out their champion to fight. Whichever man loses, their nation will become subject to the other.

As a large man with a formidable appearance, Goliath is confident of victory.

The Israelite army cowers in fear before this imposing man. No one dares to fight him. No one, that is, until young David comes along.

Full of godly confidence, David runs toward the arrogant Goliath with only his sling and five stones. Goliath mocks him for his audacity.

Yet with David slinging his first stone, Goliath falls. David uses the giant-of-a-man's own sword to behead him.

With their defeated champion lying dead in the valley, the Philistine army flees. The Israelite army gives pursuit. They rout their enemy and plunder their camp.

From a human standpoint, Goliath stands as the sure victor. Yet David prevails. Such is the case when we align ourselves with the Lord Almighty.

With God on our side, one person can make the difference.

Are we more like Goliath or like David? How well do we do at placing our confidence in God instead of our own abilities?

[Read about Goliath in 1 Samuel 17:1–54. Discover more in 1 Samuel 21:9.]

50. MERAB

King Saul has two daughters. Merab is the oldest.

When David kills Goliath, the expectation among the troops is that the king will give his oldest daughter to that man in marriage. We don't know if the men merely assume the king will do this or if that was his pledge. Regardless, he doesn't.

Later, however, Saul offers Merab as a wife for David if he'll go to war to fight the king's battles for him. But this is a ruse. Saul expects David to die in the military conflict, saving the king the trouble of killing David himself. Saul never suspects David will return victorious, but when he does, the king reneges on his promise and marries off Merab to another man, Adriel.

Saul never intended for David to marry Merab. Instead, the king uses his daughter to entice David to do something life-threatening. In this we see a father who exploits his daughter as bait to try to bring about his enemy's death.

Merab and Adriel have five sons. This is the last we hear about her. The story, however, is not over, for David has eyes for Merab's younger sister, Michal.

When have we ever made a promise we had no intention of keeping? When have we used someone else to accomplish our goals?

[Read about Merab in 1 Samuel 18:17–19. Discover more in 1 Samuel 17:25.]

51. MICHAL

King Saul's younger daughter is Michal. She loves David.

David plays a critical role in the success of King Saul and the nation of Israel. The king should be grateful, yet Saul's attitude toward David vacillates, with Saul often wanting to kill David out of jealousy.

When Saul learns that Michal loves David, the king hatches a plan to use her to bring about David's downfall. For a dowry, Saul requests proof that David has killed one hundred Philistines. Saul assumes David will die trying. Instead, David succeeds and presents evidence he's killed twice as many.

David and Michal marry.

When Michal learns of her father's latest plan to kill David, she helps her husband escape and covers for him. But when her father confronts her, she lies and says that David forced her to help him get away.

Later, when David flees for his life, Saul gives Michal to another man. Eventually, David arranges for Michal's return.

After David ascends to power, he brings the ark of the Lord back, celebrating wildly in praise to God. Michal criticizes his excessive public display of worship and despises him for his actions. Though she once loved him, she no longer does.

We can only guess why. Did his passionate celebratory dance repel her? Perhaps she gave her heart to her second husband. Or maybe it was because David married other women.

Regardless, Michal never has any children. Might David have rejected her because of her disapproval of his exuberant dance? Or maybe God punished her for criticizing David's passionate worship.

In any regard, her critical spirit is not attractive. Having a critical spirit never is.

When have we had a critical spirit? What should we do about it?

[Read about Michal in 1 Samuel 18:20–29 and 2 Samuel 6:16–23. Discover more in 1 Samuel 19:11–17 and 1 Samuel 25:44.]

52. AHIMELEK (1)

Ahimelek is a priest. He lives in Nob. One of the times when David flees for his life from King Saul, he goes to the priest in Nob.

David's unexpected arrival troubles Ahimelek. But David lies. He assures the priest everything is okay, that he's on an urgent mission for the king.

David asks Ahimelek for food and a weapon. The only food Ahimelek has is some of the consecrated bread. He gives it to David. The only weapon Ahimelek has is Goliath's sword. He gives that to David too. Then David leaves.

When Saul learns that Ahimelek helped David escape, he orders the priest's execution. While none

More Old Testament Sinners and Saints

of his men are willing to kill a priest, Doeg the Edomite has no such reluctance.

Doeg kills Ahimelek, along with all the other priests from Nob.

Only Abiathar, Ahimelek's son, escapes. He flees and joins David. When David learns what happened, he realizes he's responsible for the death of the priests.

When is lying justified? When have we suffered for doing what we thought was right?

[Read about Ahimelek in 1 Samuel 21:1–9 and 1 Samuel 22:9–23. Discover more in Psalm 52.]

53. DOEG

Doeg the Edomite appears in only one passage in Scripture. His story intertwines with Ahimelek's.

When King Saul orders the execution of Ahimelek for assisting in David's escape, none of the king's men are willing to kill the priest. They are wise to respect the function of the priesthood, and they likely realize he is innocent of what the king is accusing him of. We applaud them for doing the right thing.

Yet there is one man, a foreigner, who has no such respect for the priesthood or for what is right. He is Doeg, from Edom.

When King Saul turns to Doeg and tells him to

More Old Testament Sinners and Saints

kill Ahimelek and all the other priests, he doesn't hesitate. That day, Doeg kills eighty-five priests.

But he doesn't stop his killing spree after obeying the king's command. He takes it upon himself to travel to the city of Nob. There he kills everyone and everything in the town. This includes all the men, women, and children, along with its cattle, donkeys, and sheep. He leaves nothing alive.

Doeg is an evil man who has no respect for the priesthood and no qualm about taking a life.

When told to do something wrong, do we resist like the king's men or comply like Doeg? How well do we do at respecting our spiritual leaders and thinking the best of them?

[Read about Doeg in 1 Samuel 22:9–23. Discover more in Proverbs 6:16–19.]

54. ABNER

bner is the commander of King Saul's army. He's also Saul's first cousin. Abner serves Saul well.

After the king's death, Abner transfers his alliance to Saul's son Ish-Bosheth, making him king over all Israel in his father's place, with David ruling over Judah.

A battle rages between Israel (led by Abner) and Judah (led by Joab). During the confrontation, Joab's brother Asahel pursues Abner with determination. Abner calls back to Asahel and tells him to chase someone else instead. Asahel refuses and continues to hound Abner. Frustrated, Abner stops fleeing and thrusts the butt of his spear into Asahel's stomach, impaling him. He dies instantly.

With Joab's army pursuing Abner's, Abner calls for an end to the fighting to avoid further bloodshed. Joab agrees and commands his army to withdraw.

Later, King Ish-Bosheth accuses Abner of sleeping with his father's concubine. The text doesn't say if the charge is true or not, so we don't know if Abner is innocent or guilty.

Regardless, the allegation incenses Abner. Knowing that David is the rightful king, Abner defects to David's camp, promising to help David secure his rule over all of Israel instead of just Judah.

They have a feast, and David sends Abner away in peace to accomplish his plan.

But when Joab hears what David did, he's furious. He secretly sends for Abner. When Abner returns, Joab approaches him as if to give him a special message. Instead, Joab stabs Abner in the stomach and he dies. In doing so, Joab murders Abner to avenge Asahel's death.

How do we respond when we're accused of something? What do we think about taking revenge?

[Read about Abner in 2 Samuel 2:8–31 and 2 Samuel 3:6–37. Discover more in 2 Samuel 4:1.]

55. ISH-BOSHETH

Ish-Bosheth is the son of King Saul. After his father's death—with the help of Abner, commander of Saul's army—Ish-Bosheth assumes his father's throne. He reigns for two years.

There's little remarkable about him or his rule.

One story we have is when he confronts Abner for sleeping with his father's concubine. Though we don't know if this is a legitimate accusation or baseless, Abner reacts negatively and defects to David's side. As part of their negotiations, David asks for his wife Michal to be restored to him, even though her father—King Saul—gave her in marriage to another man.

Michal, incidentally, is Ish-Bosheth's sister. He has no qualms taking her from her current husband

and giving her back to David. We can only guess if Ish-Bosheth does this because he has no regard for his sister or because he fears Abner and David. Nonetheless, Michal is restored to David, whether she wishes it or not.

Abner's alliance with David, however, doesn't last long, for Joab murders the commander during a time of peace, in an act of revenge.

Likely unaware that Abner defected, Ish-Bosheth loses his courage when he learns his army's commander is dead. Abner brought the king into power. Without the commander to protect him, two of Ish-Bosheth's military leaders assassinate him.

Not only does Ish-Bosheth's life and reign end, so does the short rule of King Saul's descendants.

When have we falsely accused someone? When have we failed to defend our family for fear of what others might do?

[Read about Ish-Bosheth in 2 Samuel 2:8–11 and 2 Samuel 3:6–15. Discover more in 2 Samuel 4.]

56. JOAB

Joab serves as the commander of David's army. He realizes much success as a military leader, but he has some severe character issues. Here are three stories about Joab.

As we learned in the chapter about Abner, after he defects to David's camp with a plan to bring all of Israel under David's rule, Joab—unbeknownst to David—summons Abner back and stabs him to death. He does this in retaliation for Abner killing his brother in battle. Joab, however, does this during a time of peace. This makes Abner's death a murder.

Next, during Absalom's coup to seize his father's throne, David runs for his life. Even so, he tells all his men to be gentle with Absalom when they encounter him. Everyone hears David's instruction, but Joab ignores it. He kills Absalom the first chance he gets. He doesn't care that he violates the king's command.

What we don't know, however, is if Joab does this because he thinks it's in David's best interest or because Absalom chose Amasa to lead his coup and didn't tap Joab. Regardless, Absalom is dead, and David is despondent over what Joab did.

In our third story of Joab, David makes Amasa —Joab's cousin—commander for life over his army instead of Joab. This may be to express his displeasure over Joab killing Absalom contrary to David's command. Regardless of David's motivation, Joab murders Amasa during a time of peace.

Though Joab did do some good in his life, we remember him for murdering Abner and Amasa, as well as killing Absalom.

What are we known for? How can we elevate the importance of our character over our achievements?

[Read about Joab in 2 Samuel 3:26–27, 2 Samuel 18:9–17, and 2 Samuel 20:9–10. Discover more in 1 Kings 2:5–6.]

57. NATHAN (2)

Nathan is a prophet during the reign of King David. The Bible has two stories about Nathan.

When David has established his kingdom and enjoys a time of peace, he shares an idea with Nathan. He wants to build a temple for the Lord.

Nathan tells David to proceed, that God is with him.

We don't know if Nathan gave David his blessing on his own accord or if it came from God. Nevertheless, that night God speaks to Nathan, telling him that David is *not* the one to build the temple. That privilege will fall to another.

In reading God's revelation to Nathan, it first seems as though it's a forward-looking prophecy to

Jesus, who will establish a spiritual temple, one without end. Yet as we continue to read God's words, they shift into talking about a literal king who will accomplish this task.

Perhaps the prophecy refers to both Jesus and his eternal supernatural temple, as well as David's son Solomon and the physical temple he will build here on earth.

Regardless, David does not build a temple for God as he wished.

Another time Nathan confronts David by sharing a parable. It's of a rich man who steals his poor neighbor's sheep to feed guests. David is irate over the rich man's greed.

That's when Nathan reveals that David is the man in the story. Though he didn't take his neighbor's sheep, he did kill his neighbor after taking the man's wife. It's the story of David committing adultery with Bathsheba and killing her husband, Uriah, so the king can take her as his wife.

David confesses his sin. And though God forgives him, David suffers the consequences of his mistake for the rest of his life.

When have we approved of something only to have God later correct our perspective? How do we react when confronted with our sin?

[Read about Nathan in 2 Samuel 7:1–17 and 2 Samuel 12:1–25. Discover more in 1 Kings 1:7–46.]

58. TAMAR (2)

The story of Tamar is tragic. She's the beautiful daughter of King David and catches the eye of her half-brother, Amnon, who lusts for her. At the advice of his cousin, Amnon feigns illness and manipulates Tamar into his bedroom, duping David into innocently arranging the whole thing.

Once alone, Amnon grabs Tamar and solicits her. She refuses—three times. When her pleading fails to dissuade him, she talks about the implications: her disgrace and him appearing foolish and wicked. She even suggests they ask Dad for permission to marry.

Amnon won't listen. Lust drives him. He loses control and rapes her.

After this, his supposed love turns into an even more intense hate. He commands her to leave, but Tamar refuses. She says that rejecting her would be an even greater insult. Amnon has her forcibly removed from his presence.

Tamar, a victim of rape, lives in desolation with her brother Absalom.

What can we do to help the victims in our world? Who is one person we can help today?

[Read about Tamar in 2 Samuel 13:1–22. Discover more in 2 Samuel 13:23–33.]

59. AMNON (1)

Amnon is the oldest son of David. As the firstborn, we'd expect him to one day replace his father as king. Yet this is not to be. Though it may have been David's intent to make Amnon king, the young man's behavior and the consequences of what he did make it impossible.

The Bible tells us that Amnon falls in love with his half-sister Tamar. Yet the law of Moses prohibits them from having a physical relationship. Amnon doesn't care. He's obsessed. Lust overtakes him. He rapes his sister and then throws her from his bedroom as though she's disposable.

Tamar goes to live with her brother Absalom,

who takes care of her. He also looks for a way to avenge her disgrace.

Three years later, he does. He has his men kill Amnon.

Though death is a disproportionate penalty for rape, Amnon deserves punishment. In his uncontrolled lust, he ruined his sister's life, robbing her of the potential her future held. His lack of restraint also brought about his death, which precluded him the opportunity to ascend to the throne in place of his father.

Just as one moment ruined his sister's life, it also resulted in a premature end to his.

What lessons can we learn from what Amnon did? What lessons can we learn from Absalom's reaction?

[Read about Amnon in 2 Samuel 13:1–39. Discover more in 2 Samuel 3:2–3.]

60. TAMAR (3)

Tamar is the daughter of Absalom. She is most beautiful. That's all we know about her. We can assume Absalom named her after her Aunt Tamar, her father's sister whom her Uncle Amnon raped. This aunt was taken in by her dad, where she lived in desolation.

By sharing her aunt's name, Absalom's daughter Tamar is linked to the tragedy that befell her aunt. We're left to wonder if this defines her or impacts her life. Yet it must have some ramifications.

Like Tamar, our name may be in memory of someone else, which may or may not have positive implications.

Yet our name—what it means or who it's

connected to—need not dictate our future. We can pursue our own path.

Regardless of what our life is now, it need not limit what we become.

How can we live our own life, regardless of the labels people give us? How can we overcome our circumstances to become all God wants us to be?

[Read about Tamar in 2 Samuel 14:27. Discover other beautiful women in Job 42:14–15 and Esther 2:7.]

61. ABIATHAR

When Doeg the Edomite, under the order of King Saul, kills Ahimelek and eighty-five other priests, only Ahimelek's son Abiathar escapes.

Abiathar flees to David, who offers him sanctuary. Abiathar takes the ephod with him. This likely refers to the ephod Moses made for the priests to wear (Exodus 28). Symbolically, this shows the priesthood going with Abiathar and in support of David.

The ephod serves as a tool to approach God to seek his guidance. When David wants to inquire of the Lord, he tells Abiathar to bring the ephod. Abiathar seeks the Lord's guidance as prescribed. And God tells David what to do.

Much later during Absalom's coup, Abiathar and Zadok, another priest, leave Jerusalem with King David, taking the ark with them. But David sends them back to the city with the ark. There they can gather information, which their sons can relay to David. They do as instructed. Soon David's reign is restored, thanks in part to Abiathar sending him inside information.

When another of David's sons, Adonijah, conducts his coup, Abiathar aligns with him in support, but Zadok does not. This is one of the few times the two priests do not operate in unison.

After David's death, with his son Solomon firmly on the throne, the new king punishes Abiathar for his disloyalty to David. Solomon removes Abiathar from the priesthood and banishes him to his fields in Anathoth.

Though Abiathar served David well for most of his life, he didn't finish strong. He made a mistake and received punishment for it. This is the last we hear of Abiathar.

When people are disloyal, how do we determine if we're to offer mercy or punishment? What must we do to finish strong?

[Read about Abiathar in 2 Samuel 15:24–36, 1 Kings 1:7–27, and 1 Kings 2:20–27. Discover more in 1 Samuel 23:6–12 and 1 Samuel 30:7–8.]

62. ABISHAI

Abishai is the brother of Joab, commander of King David's army. Scripture tells us that Abishai is one of David's mighty warriors, a subcommander of his army, and credited with impressive military victories.

He's also zealous for David, perhaps too much so. Or maybe he has a thirst for killing and vengeance. Here are two stories that reveal his nature.

First, when David flees for his life from King Saul, he and Abishai sneak into Saul's camp undetected. With Saul asleep, Abishai sees this as an opportunity to kill David's enemy. He asks David for permission to run his spear through the king.

More Old Testament Sinners and Saints

David won't allow it. He reprimands Abishai, noting that Saul is the Lord's anointed, and they shouldn't harm him. David has confidence God will deal with Saul in his own way and timing.

Though Saul is intent on killing David, David refuses to reciprocate.

Another time, during Absalom's coup attempt, David again runs for his life. A man named Shimei curses the king as he flees, pelting him with rocks. Shimei calls David a murderer and a scoundrel.

Just as before, Abishai wants to defend David, this time by cutting off Shimei's head. Again, David rebuffs Abishai and defers to God's judgment.

Both times, David stops Abishai from being overzealous and killing another person.

Are we zealous to a fault? When has someone rebuffed us for our eagerness to act?

[Read about Abishai in 1 Samuel 26:6–11 and 2 Samuel 16:9–13. Discover more in 2 Samuel 3:30, 2 Samuel 23:18, and 1 Chronicles 18:12.]

63. HUSHAI

Hushai is an Arkite. The Bible tells us little about the Arkites, other than that they descend from Noah's grandson Canaan. This makes Hushai a foreigner in Israel, a non-Jew. Yet he is also loyal to King David, serving as his confidant.

When Absalom attempts a coup against David, the king flees for his life. Hushai aligns with David and intends to leave with him. Yet David has a different idea. He sends Hushai back to advise Absalom, with the plan to give poor advice and thwart the recommendations of Absalom's other adviser, Ahithophel.

Though this is at significant personal risk should Absalom learn of his covert activities, Hushai does

More Old Testament Sinners and Saints

as David requests. Not only does Hushai successfully thwart the advice given to Absalom by Ahithophel, but he also sends reports back to King David about Absalom's plans.

As a result of Hushai's bold actions, David escapes Absalom's grasp and later reclaims his throne.

How loyal are we to our leaders? How willing are we to take a personal risk to do something daring?

[Read about Hushai in 2 Samuel 17:5–16. Discover more in 2 Samuel 15:32–37 and 1 Chronicles 27:33.]

64. AHITHOPHEL

Ahithophel is King David's counselor. Yet when Absalom attempts his coup against his father, Ahithophel shows no sign of loyalty to David and aligns himself with Absalom.

Ahithophel gives Absalom advice, which we later find out is correct. But Hushai—working under David's direction to foil Ahithophel—provides a conflicting recommendation, albeit for David's benefit and not Absalom's. Absalom accepts Hushai's counsel and rejects Ahithophel's.

When Ahithophel realizes Absalom ignored his advice, he goes home in disgrace. Once there, he puts his estate in order and hangs himself.

How do we react when we encounter an enormous embarrassment? What other options might Ahithophel have pursued?

[Read about Ahithophel in 2 Samuel 17:1–23. Discover more in 2 Samuel 15:31–36 and 2 Samuel 16:15–23.]

65. AMASA (1)

In Absalom's brief coup attempt against his father, he appoints Amasa as commander of his rebel troops. Amasa is the first cousin of Joab, who commands David's army.

During the rebellion, Joab kills Absalom. This occurs despite David's explicit command to spare his son's life. Though doing so ends the coup and restores David to power, David mourns his son's death and is angry with Joab.

David replaces Joab as commander of his army with Amasa, giving him a lifetime appointment. This is despite Amasa aligning with Absalom and helping facilitate his rebellion.

Unfortunately, Amasa's appointment doesn't

last long. Joab murders him shortly after David promotes him.

This occurs when Joab approaches Amasa. Feigning friendship and even calling him brother, Joab plunges a dagger into the unsuspecting man's stomach. Amasa dies.

What can we learn from David promoting Amasa despite being part of Absalom's coup? How can we guard against people who act friendly toward us but will do us harm?

[Read about Amasa in 2 Samuel 17:25, 2 Samuel 19:13, and 2 Samuel 20:4–13. Discover more in 1 Kings 2:1–6.]

66. ABISHAG

Abishag is a young, beautiful Shunammite woman. She's carefully selected to attend to King David in his old age. Despite her sleeping next to him to keep him warm, their relationship isn't sexual—though I'm sure people thought otherwise.

When the king dies, we might assume her ordeal is over. But it's not. After David's death, his son Adonijah requests, through Bathsheba, that her son Solomon, the new king, allow him to marry Abishag.

Though this seems like a reasonable request, Solomon sees this as Adonijah's attempt to elevate his standing in the kingdom and vie for leadership.

More Old Testament Sinners and Saints

His perceived power struggle is a threat to Solomon's reign. So Solomon executes Adonijah.

Abishag has her life in front of her, full of expectation, when she's tapped to serve the king. Then another man tries to use her to usurp his half-brother's throne. His ploy results in his execution.

We don't know what happens to Abishag after this.

How do we react when someone uses us? How should we respond to things outside our control?

[Read about Abishag in 1 Kings 1:1–4. Discover more in 1 Kings 2:13–25.]

67. ADONIJAH (1)

David's first four sons are Amnon, Kileab, Absalom, and Adonijah. Each one has a different mother, making them all half-brothers. Absalom kills Amnon for raping their sister Tamar. Then Absalom dies in a coup attempt. The Bible only mentions Kileab once, so he likely does nothing noteworthy nor notorious.

As a result, Adonijah may think he's next in line to become king. He attempts to assume the throne, but David installs Solomon as king instead.

Fearing for his life, Adonijah begs Solomon not to kill him. Solomon offers mercy to his older half-brother, who's also the biggest threat to his rule. Solomon basically says that if Adonijah behaves

More Old Testament Sinners and Saints

himself he will live, but if he does evil, then he must die.

All is fine for Adonijah until he asks Solomon's permission to marry Abishag, their father's personal assistant.

Though we don't know Adonijah's motivation—be it for love or for power—Solomon sees his half-brother's request as a move toward taking control of the kingdom and replacing Solomon as king.

Solomon orders Adonijah's execution.

Is there ever a time when it's unwise to offer mercy? What should we use as a guideline in determining what to do?

[Read about Adonijah in 1 Kings 1:5–53 and 1 Kings 2:13–25. Discover more in 2 Samuel 3:1–5.]

68. SONS OF KORAH (2)

There are several men named Korah in the Bible. The one we know best is the Levite Korah who rebels against Moses and God. Because of the uprising he leads, God kills Korah and his family—and presumably his three sons.

Therefore, it's not likely this Korah's sons—that is, his descendants—who we read about in the book of Psalms. But if it's a different Korah, we know nothing about him.

Regardless, these "Sons of Korah" are listed in the preamble in eleven of the 150 psalms. These introductory phrases are part of the original text, unlike subheadings that were later added, as we see throughout the rest of the Bible.

Though the Sons of Korah may have written each song, an alternate interpretation is that they performed them.

To have their names attached to these eleven psalms suggests they're skilled at what they do and enjoy a following. Their praise of God is noteworthy and an example that can inspire us.

What are we known for? How can we better praise God?

[Read about the Sons of Korah in the preambles of Psalms 42, 44 through 49, 84, 85, 87, and 88. Discover more in the preambles of Psalms 3, 50, 72, 89, and 90.]

69. ZADOK (1)

Zadok and Abiathar serve David as priests. The two work together in support of him. During Absalom's coup attempt, they both side with David. The pair covertly work to send information about Absalom's short-lived reign back to David's camp through their sons.

This is not the case, however, when Adonijah tries to insert himself as his father's successor. Though Abiathar defects to align himself with Adonijah's fleeting rebellion, Zadok does not. Zadok remains loyal to King David, along with Nathan the prophet and Benaiah, son of Jehoiada.

David quells Adonijah's uprising by pronouncing Solomon as his official replacement and installing him as king. Solomon could have

More Old Testament Sinners and Saints

ordered Abiathar's execution for supporting his half-brother's rebellion, but he does not. Though Solomon notes that the priest deserves to die, the wise king allows him to live because of his earlier service to David.

Solomon does, however, remove Abiathar as priest and sends him home to live. The king replaces him with the loyal Zadok.

Zadok proves himself as a worthy priest, in part for supporting David and Solomon as God's appointed kings.

How supportive are we of our leaders? Will others celebrate our loyalty?

[Read about Zadok in 1 Kings 1:5–45 and 1 Kings 2:35. Discover more in 2 Samuel 15:24–36.]

70. QUEEN OF SHEBA

The queen of Sheba hears about the stunning reputation of King Solomon. She's skeptical and travels to meet him. The queen wants to see if there is any truth to the reports she's heard.

Presenting him with gifts, she talks with Solomon at length. The king answers her every question, able to fully explain all things to her. He impresses her. She's also astounded by what she sees.

The queen affirms his great wisdom and immense wealth, declaring that what she heard fails to communicate the fullness of all she saw and experienced. She is in awe.

More Old Testament Sinners and Saints

Solomon loads her up with gifts, and she returns home.

The queen of Sheba had to see to believe.

Do we have the faith to believe without seeing? How far will we go to discover what is true?

[Read about the queen of Sheba in 1 Kings 10:1–13. Discover more in Luke 11:29–31.]

71. AGUR

We commonly think of King Solomon as the author of the book of Proverbs. While this is mostly true, it's not completely correct. Proverbs also contains wisdom from Agur (as well as Lemuel, whom we'll cover in a bit).

Agur is the son of Jakeh. Neither man, however, appears anywhere else in Scripture, so we know nothing more about them from the biblical account. Yet what Agur writes does reveal his practical insights.

Sandwiched between his opening praises to God and his ending plethora of wise insights, is a key consideration.

He asks God for two things.

More Old Testament Sinners and Saints

First is that God will keep falsehood and lies at bay. We can see this as him wanting protection from the untruths of others, as well as to not spread them himself.

His second request is that God will give him neither poverty nor wealth. He merely asks for his daily bread.

Though this may seem like a strange petition, he explains his rationale.

He worries that if he is satiated, he may turn from God, feeling a smug self-satisfaction. His counter concern is that if he has too little, he may steal to provide for his needs.

He wants to avoid both extremes. So asking for his daily bread, neither less nor more, is his petition.

What can we learn from Agur's two requests? Should we share his concern about not having enough or alternately of having too much?

[Read about Agur in Proverbs 30. Discover more in Matthew 6:9–13.]

72. LEMUEL

Immediately after the proverbs of Agur, we have the proverbs of Lemuel. The Bible refers to him as King Lemuel. Yet his name doesn't appear elsewhere in Scripture, so we don't know what he's the king of.

Nor do we know anything else about him, aside from his wise sayings. Yet even this label misleads us. What follows this grand introduction are not the sayings of Lemuel, but instead the words of his mother.

In this brief passage of only nine verses, he merely preserves her words for us to read today, but we should be glad he did.

There are two primary thoughts in these proverbs from King Lemuel's mom.

More Old Testament Sinners and Saints

First is a warning to stay away from wine and beer, lest they impair our memory. Beer is for the perishing, while wine is for those in anguish.

Second is the reminder to speak for those who cannot speak for themselves, to stand up for the destitute and judge fairly.

King Lemuel has a wise mother, and he is wise for recording her wisdom for us to read.

What have our parents taught us that we need to share with others? What can we pass on to the next generation?

[Read about Lemuel in Proverbs 31:1–9. Discover more in Proverbs 1:8–9.]

73. REHOBOAM

After King Solomon dies, his son Rehoboam succeeds him as king. Jeroboam opposes him.

Jeroboam, one of Solomon's officials, had received a prophetic word that he would become king over ten of the tribes of Israel, with Solomon's descendants ruling over the tribe of Judah.

Jeroboam, along with all of Israel, approach Rehoboam with a request. They ask him to lighten the people's load. If he does, they'll surely serve him.

Wisely, Rehoboam asks for three days to consider it.

The king seeks advice from the elders who had served Solomon during his reign. They think

More Old Testament Sinners and Saints

Jeroboam's request makes sense and recommend that Rehoboam agree to it.

But Rehoboam doesn't like their advice. He consults with his peers, young men he grew up with and who were now serving him as king. They give him the opposite counsel. This is what Rehoboam wants to hear.

Jeroboam and the people return in three days to learn Rehoboam's response. The king doesn't give them a favorable answer. He refuses to lighten their load. Instead, he'll do the opposite. He'll demand even more of them than his father.

The people reject Rehoboam as king and follow Jeroboam. Rehoboam is left with only the tribe of Judah to rule over, just as the prophet predicted.

Who should we get advice from? What do we do when we receive counsel we don't like?

[Read about Rehoboam in 1 Kings 12:1–24. Discover more in 1 Kings 14:21–31 and Matthew 1:7.]

74. ASA

Asa is the king of Judah. He's the son of Abijah, the son of Rehoboam, the son of Solomon, the son of David. This means Asa is King David's great-great-grandson.

He reigns for forty-one years. Scripture says he does what is right in God's eyes. And he remains fully committed to the Lord throughout his life. This is the opposite of his father, Abijah, who served as an evil king.

Asa rids the land of idol worship and deposes his grandmother Maakah from her position as queen mother for her worship of Asherah. He brings about much needed spiritual reform to the nation of Judah during his rule.

Even so, his reign as king is marked by a

More Old Testament Sinners and Saints

continual war against Israel. This shows us that doing what is right and honoring God doesn't guarantee a life absent of conflict.

There's one more thing we can affirm Asa for. He raises his son, Jehoshaphat, well. Like his father, Jehoshaphat does what is right and follows the Lord. This is unlike so many of the other kings of Judah who do not prepare their sons to rule in a God- honoring way.

We applaud Asa for serving God as he leads the people of Judah and for raising his son to do the same.

When we do what is right, do we expect God to bless us with a comfortable life? What are we doing to prepare the next generation to serve the Lord?

[Read about Asa in 1 Kings 15:8–24 and 1 Kings 22:41–44. Discover more in Matthew 1:8.]

75. OBADIAH (4)

Obadiah is a devout believer of God. (He is not the prophet Obadiah, who lives much later.) The Bible contains only one story about this Obadiah, who serves as palace administrator for the evil King Ahab.

During the time of Ahab, king of Israel, there's a three-year drought, which produces a famine. This is as the prophet Elijah proclaimed.

King Ahab's wife, Jezebel, strives to kill all the prophets of God. Yet Obadiah protects one hundred of them, hiding them in two caves. And despite there being a drought and famine, he also supplies them with food and water. He does this at great personal risk, for if Queen Jezebel finds out what he's doing, she'll surely kill him.

In the middle of this, Ahab dispatches Obadiah to search for springs of water and grass to feed his horses and mules.

As Obadiah goes about his assignment, he meets Elijah. Obadiah bows before the prophet.

Then Obadiah asks a curious question: "What have I done wrong?"

For the past three years, King Ahab has been conducting an unsuccessful manhunt for Elijah. Obadiah fears that when he reports Elijah's whereabouts to the king, God's Spirit will whisk the prophet away to another place. Obadiah worries the king will kill him in frustration for giving a false report.

Elijah promises he won't disappear. He pledges he'll come before King Ahab that very day.

Obadiah tells Ahab where Elijah is, and the king goes out to meet him. A huge showdown is about to take place between Elijah and the prophets of Baal.

What great personal risk are we willing to take to serve God? What lessons can we learn from Obadiah?

[Read about Obadiah in 1 Kings 18:1–16. Discover more in 1 Kings 17:1 and 1 Kings 18:17–40.]

76. GEHAZI

Gehazi is the servant of Elisha.

The first time we encounter Gehazi is in the story about the Shunammite woman. When her only son dies, she seeks Elisha. Elisha gives his staff to Gehazi and dispatches him. He instructs his servant to rush to the boy and lay the staff on his face.

Gehazi does as instructed, but the child doesn't come back to life.

When Elisha arrives at the woman's home, he raises the boy from the dead. He sends Gehazi to call the boy's mother. Elisha presents her with her son, now very much alive.

The second time we read about Gehazi is in the

story of Elisha healing Naaman of leprosy. When Naaman does as Elisha instructed, his skin is restored, and the leprosy is gone.

Yet Elisha won't accept any of the gifts Naaman offers.

Thinking that Elisha is wrong to refuse Naaman's generosity, Gehazi runs after Naaman. He lies to the man, asking for money and clothes. Naaman gladly gives what he requested and more.

Gehazi receives the gifts and hides them in his house.

When Elisha confronts Gehazi, the servant denies any wrongdoing. Yet in his spirit, Elijah saw exactly what happened.

As punishment, Elisha curses Gehazi—and his descendants forever—with Naaman's leprosy. Gehazi's skin turns white with a leprous infection.

Though we don't know if Gehazi is to blame for not being able to raise the Shunammite woman's son from the dead, we do know he failed. And when he went against Elisha's wishes to get some of Naaman's gifts and then lied about it, he received punishment for his actions.

When have we reacted selfishly or out of greed? What consequences of our sins will affect future generations?

[Read about Gehazi in 2 Kings 4:11–37 and 2 Kings 5:19–27. Discover more in 2 Kings 8:1–5.]

77. ZECHARIAH (1)

We find many men throughout Scripture named Zechariah. The Bible may have more Zechariahs in it than any other name. With many obscure mentions throughout the Bible—fifty-nine times in nine books—it's impossible to determine accurately how many there are, but there are perhaps as many as twenty-two men named Zechariah in Scripture.

The main three are Zechariah (1), the king of Israel; Zechariah (15), the prophet, and Zechariah (22), the father of John the Baptist.

Zechariah (1) is notable because he's the first one mentioned in Scripture. He is a king of Israel—and evil.

More Old Testament Sinners and Saints

He is the son of Jeroboam II, the son of Jehoash, the son of Jehoahaz, the son of Jehu. They are all kings of Israel. We'll see shortly why this is significant.

Zechariah—like all the kings of Israel after the nation split in two—is a sinful king. He does evil in the Lord's eyes, as did his predecessors. His reign lasts only six months. Shallum assassinates him, then replaces him as king. Interestingly, Shallum's reign is even shorter, lasting just one month, when he is likewise assassinated.

Though some evil kings enjoyed a long reign, Zechariah does not.

Before Zechariah's great-great-grandfather—Jehu—becomes king, he kills all King Ahab's descendants, along with his chiefs, close friends, and priests. No one survives. Then Jehu kills all the prophets of Baal and destroys their temple.

Jehu's actions please God and accomplish all God intended to do to the house of the evil king Ahab. Therefore, God promises Jehu that his descendants will rule to the fourth generation.

Despite this promising start, however, Jehu fails to keep God's laws with his whole heart. He continues the sins of former kings.

Even so, God fulfills his promise to Jehu that his

reign will continue for four generations. Zechariah is the fourth. They are all evil.

What might we enjoy—even though undeserved—because of something one of our ancestors did? What are we doing to build on our lives for future generations?

[Read about Zechariah in 2 Kings 15:8–12. Discover more in 2 Kings 10:1–35, 2 Kings 13:9, 2 Kings 14:16, and 2 Kings 14:29.]

78. JOSIAH (1)

Josiah is a child when he becomes king, a mere eight years old. He rules for thirty-one years and does right in God's eyes, just as his ancestor King David had done.

Eight years into his reign, which makes him sixteen, he seeks God, just like David. Four years later, he purges the nation of idol worship. In his eighteenth year as king, he sets about to purify the land and the temple.

He orders that the offerings given at the temple be used to repair it. While doing the renovations, the high priest finds the Book of the Law in the temple. While we don't know how long God's Word had been misplaced, its contents surprise Josiah and all the people as something they had no knowledge of.

Upon hearing its words, Josiah tears his clothes in agony to display his remorse over what prior generations had done in disobeying God and disrespecting his worship. He sends his aides to consult with the prophetess Huldah to seek the Lord over what to do.

She confirms that God will indeed enforce the punishment warned about in the book for the people's persistent rebellion against him. Yet because Josiah had humbled himself before God, the Lord promises that the king will not witness destruction during his lifetime. He will see peace.

The promised punishment will happen later. But it will happen—just as God had already done to the nation of Israel to punish them for their ongoing sins.

Then Josiah celebrates Passover like never before, something not seen during the time of the kings or even the time of the judges. It's an extravagant observance lasting seven days.

How do we expect God to respond when we humble ourselves

before him? What can we do to celebrate God and worship him more fully?

[Read about Josiah in 2 Chronicles 34–35. Discover more in 1 Kings 13:2 and 2 Kings 22–23.]

79. AMOS (1)

Chronologically, Amos follows Jonah and slightly overlaps with Hosea. He's also a contemporary of Isaiah. Occupationally he works as a shepherd and doesn't think of himself as a prophet.

In fact, he confirms to the priest Amaziah that he isn't a prophet nor the son of a prophet. Yet God told him to prophesy, so he did. When God called him, he was tending a flock and caring for sycamore-fig trees.

Amos proclaims God's truth during the reigns of kings Uzziah of Judah and Jeroboam II of Israel. He foretells judgment on many nations, including Judah, but Israel receives his primary focus.

In general, his message to all the nations is that they have sinned, and God will punish them.

Through all this, Amos is faithful to God's call on his life and ministry.

Do we need credentials to serve God? When he calls us to do something, do we tell him we're not able or do we say yes?

[Read about Amos in Amos 1:1 and Amos 7:14–15. Discover a parallel story in Matthew 9:9.]

80. HOSEA

God speaks to Hosea, son of Beeri. The Almighty calls the young man to be his prophet. In a shocking move, however, God tells Hosea to marry a prostitute.

God doesn't tell Hosea which prostitute to marry. Hosea gets to choose. We don't know his selection criteria, but he picks Gomer. They marry, but they don't have a happy life as husband and wife.

They have a son. Then Gomer has two more children, but the subtext suggests Hosea doubts he's their father.

God prompts Hosea to use his relationship with Gomer and her illegitimate offspring as sermon illustrations in his scathing rebuke against the nations of Israel and Judah for their unfaithfulness to God.

This may embarrass Gomer, or maybe she's bored. Regardless, she runs off and takes up with another lover.

Yet God tells Hosea to go after her and bring her home. Hosea finds Gomer. He must buy her back, that is, he redeems her. Then he tells her to stop running around, to be faithful to only him. In doing so he offers her undeserved love and even accepts her two kids who were likely fathered by other men.

Hosea married Gomer even though she was undeserving. And he offered her redeeming love when she ran away.

So it is with God and us.

How willing are we to obey God when he tells us to do something outrageous? What if it's something we don't want to do or is painful?

[Read about Hosea in Hosea 1–3. Discover more in Romans 9:25–26.]

81. GOMER (2)

Gomer is a prostitute. We can assume she offers her body to other men to ensure her survival: food, water, and clothes. Or perhaps she's merely promiscuous.

Either way, she isn't marriage material. Yet, God's prophet Hosea marries her anyway.

Gomer and Hosea have a son, Jezreel.

Then she has two more children, but Hosea questions if he is their father. One is a girl, Lo-Ruhamah. The other is a boy, Lo-Ammi.

After that, unfaithful Gomer abandons her husband and three children. She runs away and takes up with another lover.

Shockingly, Hosea goes after her. The prophet buys her freedom. He tells her to stop chasing other

More Old Testament Sinners and Saints

men, to return home, and to be faithful to him. He offers her a love she doesn't deserve.

Hosea married Gomer even though she didn't deserve it. Later he redeemed her after she left him for another man.

Hosea's astonishing actions toward the sinful Gomer hint at God's unconditional love for us. And Gomer's lifestyle reminds us that we are all sinful people, undeserving of Jesus redeeming us and becoming his pure, spotless bride.

How can we move beyond our past to accept God's unconditional love for us? How does knowing that God has already forgiven our sins help us to forgive ourselves?

[Read about Gomer in Hosea 1:2–8 and Hosea 3:1–3. Discover more in Romans 5:8.]

82. JEZREEL

Jezreel is the first son of Hosea and Gomer. His name is an allusion to a place called Jezreel. Though there are many people in the Bible who have a place named after them, this may be the first time in Scripture we see a person named after a place.

What happened in Jezreel is notorious. This is where the overzealous—or perhaps power-hungry—Jehu slays all who remain in the family of evil king Ahab. He also murders the king's advisors, close friends, and priests. Though God wants Ahab punished for his ungodly behavior, there's no hint this extends to his counselors, friends, and priests.

The arrival of Hosea's son foreshadows the impending arrival of God's punishment on the

More Old Testament Sinners and Saints

nation of Israel, ending their existence as a country. Though the stated reason for this judgment is Jehu's massacre, what he did represents the nation's repeated rejection of God over several centuries.

Jezreel's birth signals the end of the nation of Israel.

What does our name mean? How do we react to having that connection?

[Read about Jezreel in Hosea 1:4–5. Discover more in 2 Kings 10:11 and Hosea 2:21–23.]

83. LO-RUHAMAH

Lo-Ruhamah is the daughter of Gomer, likely the result of adultery. Her mom, a former prostitute, cheats on her husband, Hosea, and has an affair with someone more appealing.

As directed by God, Hosea names his wife's illegitimate child. He calls her Lo-Ruhamah, which means *no pity* or *not loved*. Yet we understand why he rejects Lo-Ruhamah, whom someone else fathered.

What a terrible label to have attached to you. What a condemning legacy to carry. Every time someone says her name, it serves as a painful reminder to Lo-Ruhamah of being rejected by the only man in her life.

Eventually Hosea reconciles with his wife and

More Old Testament Sinners and Saints

accepts Lo-Ruhamah as his daughter. At last, he offers her love.

We wonder how Lo-Ruhamah responds. Does she rise above the shameful circumstance of her conception, or does she remain forever wounded by what her mother did?

Whether many or few, we all carry wounds from our parents. Yet we are wrong to blame them for our issues. Though we don't choose our parents, we can choose how we respond to their mistakes in raising us.

What issue in our lives do we blame on others? How can we trust God to help us move beyond our past and not be held captive by it?

[Read about Lo-Ruhamah in Hosea 1:6 and Hosea 2:23. Discover more in Romans 5:8.]

84. LO-AMMI

Lo-Ammi is the son of Gomer. Given what his name means, he is also the result of adultery, just like Lo-Ruhamah. He may have the same biological father as Lo-Ruhamah, or they may have different dads. Regardless, Hosea is not his father.

Again, it is God who gives him his name, not his mother, biological father, or stepdad. The name Lo-Ammi means *not my people*, which carries a double implication.

In a direct way, his name reminds all that Hosea is not his father. Each time Hosea calls to Lo-Ammi, he effectively says, "Come here, 'son who is not mine'."

More importantly, there is a deeper spiritual

meaning, which is God's focus. In this way, Lo-Ammi personifies God's people. Because of their repeated rejection of God, he will reject them. He will disown them, saying, "You are not my people."

Yet he will only turn from them for a time. He looks forward to the day when he can change their name from "You are not my people" (that is, Lo-Ammi), to "children of the living God."

What name does God have for us as an individual? How can we better embrace the truth that as Jesus's followers we are children of the living God?

[Read about Lo-Ammi in Hosea 1:8–10 and Hosea 2:23. Discover more in 1 John 3:1.]

85. MICAH (5)

The prophet Micah is a contemporary of Isaiah. Micah's ministry overlaps and follows Hosea's. We know little else about Micah from the Bible except that he comes from Moresheth, but Scripture doesn't reveal where it is.

Micah prophesies to the nations of Israel and Judah during the reigns of several kings: Jotham, Ahaz, and Hezekiah of Judah.

He delivers strong words from God. This should convict the people, but it doesn't. Instead, they take offense. The other prophets—false prophets—tell Micah to stop talking, as if his silence will keep God's plans from happening.

Micah responds with sarcasm, saying that if a prophet proclaimed plenty of wine and beer for all, the people would flock to him. Rather than accept the truth, the people prefer to anesthetize themselves from it.

Telling the people what they want to hear—as opposed to what is true—is making a false prophecy. When the prophets don't say what the people want to hear, the people turn against them. This is a consumeristic mindset, embracing what's pleasant, even if it's wrong.

It happened to Micah. It happened to Jesus. And it still happens today.

How willing are we to share God's truth with others? How do we react when we face opposition?

[Read about Micah in Micah 1:1–2 and Micah 2:6. Discover more in Jeremiah 26:18.]

86. NAHUM (1)

Following closely after Micah and Isaiah is Nahum. Nahum is an Elkoshite. He only appears once in the Bible, so we know nothing else about him from Scripture.

We do, however, know his message. He prophesies destruction against the city of Nineveh and the nation of Assyria, just like Jonah did about a century earlier. Back then the people received Jonah's lackluster message and repented.

This time the people of Nineveh do not.

We know that God used Assyria to punish Israel for them repeatedly turning away from him. This doesn't suggest Assyria is a good nation or favored by God. In his omnipotence, he uses them to accomplish what he had warned his people would happen.

Though some may think God unfair to punish Assyria for accomplishing his purpose, that's exactly what he will do. Nahum makes this clear when he declares that God opposes Nineveh, the capital of Assyria.

Just because Assyria fulfilled God's will doesn't mean it found favor with him or that he will spare the nation from punishment for the evil it did.

Is it too much of a stretch to consider that we could do God's will but still fall short of his expectations and therefore receive punishment?

We can't secure our salvation by what we do. We can't earn eternity through our behavior.

Instead, we realize salvation when we follow Jesus and believe in him to save us.

What are we doing to try to earn God's favor and salvation? Does God owe us anything when we do his will?

[Read about Nahum in Nahum 1:1. Discover more in Ephesians 2:8–9.]

87. ZEPHANIAH (1)

Following Nahum is the prophet Zephaniah. The only information the Bible gives us about Zephaniah is his parentage and that he prophesies during the reign of King Josiah. Zephaniah is the son of Cushi, grandson of Gedaliah, great-grandson of Amariah, and great-great-grandson of Hezekiah. But knowing his lineage gives us no more insight into his person.

Zephaniah's prophetic words address an array of nations, including Judah and exiled Israel, with many more countries, along with the entire world. He also has a stinging rebuke for the people's spiritual leaders, a warning which we all—leaders and laity alike—should take seriously and diligently guard against.

Despite all this, Zephaniah ends his prophecy with hope for the people. Though they live in a difficult era and the immediate future is bleak, there will come a time when God will gather his people and bring them home. He will give them honor and praise from all the inhabitants throughout the earth.

And that's something to anticipate.

When we struggle, do we focus on our present trials or look forward to a better tomorrow? Regardless of our situation, do we place our confidence in the Lord?

[Read about Zephaniah in Zephaniah 1:1. Discover more in Zephaniah 3:4 & 20.]

88. OBADIAH (8)

The Bible has *nine* men with the name Obadiah, but the prophet is the best known among them. Overlapping Habakkuk and following him is Obadiah. His one-chapter book in the Bible records what God reveals to him in a vision.

He likely lives in Judah. His prophecy addresses the nation of Edom, descendants of Esau. Because he is a contemporary of Habakkuk, the prophet's ministry may occur during the reigns of Jehoiachin or Zedekiah.

Among other things, Obadiah criticizes Edom for its pride. The primary issue, however, is not what the people of Edom did but what they didn't do. When foreign armies attacked Jerusalem, they

More Old Testament Sinners and Saints

did nothing to help. They stood aloof and watched (Obadiah 1:11).

Theirs is not an act of commission, but of omission. Their sin is inaction.

In what ways are we proud today? What are our sins of inaction?

[Read about Obadiah in Obadiah 1:1. Discover more in Proverbs 16:18 and 1 John 2:16.]

89. HABAKKUK

Following Zephaniah by a few years is Habakkuk. He is the only person named Habakkuk in the Bible, and he only appears in his book of prophecy. His ministry overlaps Jeremiah's and most of Obadiah's. He prophesies just before Judah's fall to Babylon.

Unlike the other prophets' writings, however, Habakkuk's book records a dialogue between him and God, with God's response emerging as prophecy.

Habakkuk complains to God. It reads like a lament. Then God responds. Next, Habakkuk issues a second complaint. Again, God responds.

Habakkuk doesn't complain a third time.

Instead, he concludes with a lengthy prayer that reads like a psalm.

We may identify with Habakkuk's grumbles to God.

His two best-known objections are in Habakkuk 1:5 and Habakkuk 2:3–4. New Testament writers quote both. Acts 13:41 references the first passage, while Romans 1:17, Galatians 3:11, and Hebrews 10:37–38 cover the second.

Yet we might do better to focus on the end of his prayer, as found in Habakkuk 3:18–19. Despite his discouragement, Habakkuk pledges to rejoice in the Lord and express joy in God, his Savior.

May we do the same.

Though God hears our complaints, might we grumble to him too often? What can we do to better rejoice in our Lord and Savior?

[Read about Habakkuk in Habakkuk 1:1–2. Discover more in Psalm 35:9.]

90. SHADRACH, MESHACH, AND ABEDNEGO

When Babylon conquers Judah, Daniel and his three friends—Hananiah, Mishael, and Azariah—are seized. They're deported to Babylon. Their names may be unfamiliar to you. That's because this trio is better known by the names given to them by their captors: Shadrach, Meshach, and Abednego.

We read of Shadrach, Meshach, and Abednego only in the book of Daniel. They always appear as a trio and never as individuals. Therefore, we'll consider them as a unit, a team. Recall the wise words of King Solomon that a cord of three strands is not easily broken (Ecclesiastes 4:12).

So it is with Shadrach, Meshach, and Abednego. Together they are strong.

In Babylon, King Nebuchadnezzar erects a monument of gold and decrees that everyone should bow before it and worship the image. The punishment for failure to do this is being burned alive.

Shadrach, Meshach, and Abednego refuse to bow.

When Nebuchadnezzar confronts them, they boldly confirm that they will not worship the image. Instead, they'll stay true to their God who is able to save them from the king's fiery furnace of death. They proclaim confidence that God will rescue them, but even if he doesn't, they'll still worship him only.

Nebuchadnezzar orders that Shadrach, Meshach, and Abednego be bound and thrown into the furnace. The fire is so hot that the guards who toss them in die. Yet Shadrach, Meshach, and Abednego do not.

The king is astounded to see the three of them walking around in the furnace, unbound and unharmed. With them is a fourth man, whom Nebuchadnezzar says looks like "a son of the gods."

The king calls them to come forth. When Shadrach, Meshach, and Abednego emerge, they're unaffected by the inferno. Their hair is not singed, their robes are not seared, and they don't smell like smoke.

Amazed, Nebuchadnezzar praises their God, even though the king doesn't know who their God is. Nebuchadnezzar decrees that anyone who says a word against the God of Shadrach, Meshach, and Abednego must die.

How willing are we to die for our faith? Who can we join as a "cord of three strands" to live a strong, God-honoring life?

[Read about Shadrach, Meshach, and Abednego in Daniel 3. Discover more in Daniel 1:6–7 & 19.]

91. NEBUCHADNEZZAR

When I consider Nebuchadnezzar, the king of Babylon, I think of an evil man who killed countless people and plundered the nations he conquered. Yet, despite his many shortfalls, I wonder if God views him differently.

Jeremiah quotes the Lord as calling Nebuchadnezzar "my servant." God plans to use Nebuchadnezzar to exact judgment on the nation of Judah for their ongoing disregard for him and his commands. This is exactly what happens. Therefore, it shouldn't surprise us to see God at work in Nebuchadnezzar's life.

Here are three stories, all from the book of Daniel:

First, Nebuchadnezzar has a dream. He believes the dream has meaning, but it confounds him. He calls all the wise people in his realm to explain it to him. Yet he refuses to tell them the dream. To verify their interpretation is correct, he requires them to first tell him the dream and then clarify what it means. If they don't have the discernment to know the dream, how can he trust their explanation?

But no one can tell Nebuchadnezzar his dream.

Then Daniel comes forward, confirming that he can't either but acknowledging that God will reveal it to him. He tells the king his dream and interprets it.

Relieved, Nebuchadnezzar honors Daniel and gives him rule over the entire province of Babylon. The king affirms God as the God of gods and King of kings, one who reveals mysteries. This is quite a proclamation for a pagan ruler to make.

Our second story about Nebuchadnezzar is the one we covered in the chapter about Shadrach, Meshach, and Abednego. The king makes a giant statue for the people to worship and decrees that anyone who fails to do so will be burned to death. The trio refuses, but God delivers them from the deadly blaze unscathed.

Amazed, Nebuchadnezzar praises God and

More Old Testament Sinners and Saints

decrees that anyone who talks against God will face a gruesome death and have their house destroyed. This is quite amazing for a king who doesn't know God.

Our last story is about another dream Nebuchadnezzar has. Daniel's interpretation reveals that, because of the king's pride, he will go insane as punishment. After seven years his sanity will return, and he'll resume his rule.

Everything happens as Daniel declared.

Upon being returned to his rule, Nebuchadnezzar praises "the Most Holy God," giving him honor and glory. He pens not one, but two passages that praise God for his infinite rule and unsurpassed power. Each reads much like a psalm.

Imagine that. Nebuchadnezzar—the nemesis of God's people—praising the Lord most high through two psalms.

In these three stories, the evil King Nebuchadnezzar emerges as an enigma. Seeing how God interacts with him—and the king's response—fills me with awe and wonder.

How open are we to see God at work in people we view as wicked? If an evil king can affirm God's power, what can we do?

[Read about Nebuchadnezzar in Daniel 1:1–2 and Daniel 2–3. Discover more in 2 Kings 24–25 and Jeremiah 25:8–9.]

92. BELSHAZZAR

Belshazzar succeeds his father Nebuchadnezzar as ruler over Babylon. Once established, he throws a grand party for one thousand of his nobles. While drinking wine —perhaps too much—he orders that the goblets taken from the temple in Jerusalem be brought out to serve his guests. In doing so, they praise their gods of gold and silver, of bronze, iron, wood, and stone.

Suddenly fingers from a disembodied hand appear and write four words on the wall. Belshazzar is understandably frightened. His face turns pale, and his knees grow weak.

He must know what it says, but no one can read

the words or decipher its meaning. At the suggestion of the queen, he calls for Daniel, promising grand rewards if Daniel can interpret the message.

Daniel dismisses the king's offer and instead chastises him.

Despite knowing what happened to Nebuchadnezzar when he became proud, Belshazzar repeated his father's error. He refused to humble himself.

Daniel reads the words and interprets them: "Your days are numbered. I repeat, your days are numbered. You've been judged and fall short. Your kingdom will be taken from you and given to the Medes and Persians."

That night Belshazzar is killed, and his kingdom is taken over by Darius, the Mede.

Though Nebuchadnezzar received a warning and a second chance, Belshazzar did not. This is perhaps because he should have known better.

What must we do to avoid committing the same mistakes as our parents? Though God is a God of mercy, are we wrong to assume he'll always give us a second chance?

[Read about Belshazzar in Daniel 5. Discover more in Daniel 7:1 and Daniel 8:1.]

93. DARIUS

When Darius becomes king in place of Belshazzar, he establishes a hierarchy to help him rule, with Daniel as one of three administrators overseeing 120 province governors. Daniel conducts himself so well that the king plans to set him over the entire kingdom.

The other two administrators and the province governors, however, don't want this. But they cannot find any way to discredit Daniel, for his work is beyond fault.

Instead, they seek to attack him through his beliefs and practices. They maneuver Darius into issuing a decree that, for one month, the people can only pray to him and no other. The king foolishly agrees.

More Old Testament Sinners and Saints

Daniel disregards this new law and continues to pray to God as usual. His detractors catch him and insist the king throw Daniel into a den of hungry lions.

Darius doesn't want to, but he has no choice. He cannot change the law. He gives the order, hoping God will rescue Daniel. In the morning, he finds that this is exactly what happened, with God shutting the lions' mouths and Daniel being unharmed. He has Daniel removed from the den and his detractors thrown in instead. The lions quickly kill them.

Then this pagan ruler does something surprising. He issues another decree, that the people must fear and reverence the God of Daniel. The king praises God and exalts him.

This would have never happened had Daniel not risked his life to do what was right.

How can we protect ourselves from being maneuvered into doing something we shouldn't do? How much are we willing to risk to worship God?

[Read about Darius in Daniel 6. Discover more in Daniel 9:1 and Daniel 11:1.]

94. ZERUBBABEL

As we read the genealogy of Jesus in Matthew 1, we read many familiar names in the first eleven verses. After the nation is exiled to Babylon, we see many unfamiliar names. But one name pops out. It is Zerubbabel, whom the Bible identifies as the son of Shealtiel.

Zerubbabel is the great-grandson of Josiah, the last God-honoring king of Judah. This means that Zerubbabel has royal blood in him. He's a descendant of David and an ancestor of Jesus.

It's after Josiah's death that Nebuchadnezzar conquers Judah and deports the people. This means Zerubbabel is born in Babylonian captivity. But he gets to return to his ancestral home when King Cyrus allows the people to go back to Judah.

With Zerubbabel being part of David's line, it's not surprising for him to assume a lead role and serve as governor, even though there is no nation for him to rule as king.

Under Zerubbabel's leadership, the people restore the altar in the destroyed temple and resume sacrifices as prescribed by Moses. Zerubbabel also begins rebuilding the temple, but legal opposition arises and halts progress.

The prophet Haggai addresses this, as does the prophet Zechariah. And even though Zechariah prophesies that Zerubbabel will complete the temple, the Bible does not confirm this. Scripture credits Ezra with rebuilding the temple (though Zerubbabel is likely present and may have been involved with it).

After Ezra completes the temple, Nehemiah rebuilds the wall around Jerusalem. But this all starts with Zerubbabel rebuilding the altar and restoring right worship.

What might God be telling us to rebuild or restore? How do we respond when we face opposition to completing what God has called us to do?

[Read about Zerubbabel in Ezra 3:2, Ezra 4:1–3, and Ezra 5:1–2. Discover more in Haggai 1–2, Zechariah 4:9–10, and Matthew 1:11–12.]

95. HAGGAI

Haggai is the first prophet to emerge after the people of Judah return home from captivity. He's also a preacher. He ministers after some Hebrew exiles in Babylon are repatriated under the decree of King Darius.

Haggai is a contemporary of Zechariah and Ezra, along with Zerubbabel. He also has a two-chapter book that contains his prophecy. It's called Haggai. Notably, the writers of Hebrews quote Haggai 2:6 in Hebrews 12:26.

Haggai chastises God's people who live in fine homes while the temple—the Almighty's home here on earth—sits in shambles.

God tries to get his people's attention for years,

but they continue to miss it. Each year they plant much but harvest little. They struggle to survive.

God wants them to rebuild his temple and reestablish it as their center of worship. He wants his people to put him first and think about their own needs second. When they do this, he will provide for them.

Ezra remarks that the people prosper under the preaching of Haggai, a fine tribute to his effectiveness as God's messenger.

If we feel we aren't receiving God's blessings, it's up to us to determine why. Do we need to reorder our priorities, or do we need to allow our Lord to grow himself in us, preparing us for the future?

Is seeking God and doing his will our first priority? What do others say about our work?

[Read about Haggai in Ezra 5:1 and Ezra 6:14. Discover more in Haggai 1–2.]

96. ZECHARIAH (15)

As mentioned in the chapter on Zechariah (1), there are many men in the Bible with the name Zechariah. The main three are Zechariah (1), the king of Israel; Zechariah (15), the prophet; and Zechariah (22), the father of John the Baptist.

Zechariah (15) is the son of Berekiah and a descendant of Iddo. Just like Haggai, Zechariah is a prophet and preacher in the land of Judah after some Hebrew exiles return home under the decree of King Darius. Zechariah is also a shepherd.

Zechariah's prophecies occur in the fourteen-chapter book that bears his name. It's the longest book of all the Minor Prophets. Three New

Testament writers—Matthew, Mark, and John—quote from the book of Zechariah.

Though the name Zechariah shows up in seven verses in the book of Nehemiah, which chronologically follows Ezra, these reference several other men with the same name and don't likely refer to the prophet Zechariah.

The book of Ezra covers what happens with the repatriated people, with both Zechariah and Haggai joining together in their prophecies. They also teach the people. Under their encouragement, along with the leadership of Ezra, the Hebrew people rebuild the temple.

Zerubbabel rebuilt the altar. Now the people have rebuilt the temple. What's next is rebuilding the wall around the city, which will fall to Nehemiah.

When have our words encouraged others to act? How can we build on the work of those who went before us or complete work for others to build upon?

[Read about Zechariah in Ezra 5:1 and Ezra 6:14. Discover more in Zechariah 1:1–6.]

97. CYRUS

In the chapters on Nebuchadnezzar and Darius, we see them both praising God. Not being Jewish or believing in the Almighty, their declarations surprise us. Yet there's more. King Cyrus also issues an unexpected proclamation.

God moves Cyrus's heart to allow the people of Judah—whom Nebuchadnezzar captured and relocated—to return home and rebuild the temple. He even supplies provisions for the people to complete their task.

Cyrus feels called by God—divinely appointed—to accomplish this task. In this we see a humility in Cyrus that both Nebuchadnezzar and Belshazzar lacked.

Though the people face significant opposition

when they return to rebuild the temple, along with much drama, they eventually restore their house of worship.

And this wouldn't have happened without God first moving the heart of King Cyrus to act.

How is God moving in our hearts today? What is he calling us to do?

[Read about Cyrus in Ezra 1:1–6 and Ezra 6:2–18. Discover more in 2 Chronicles 36:22–23 and Isaiah 45:1–13.]

98. XERXES

King Xerxes is a powerful ruler, but he doesn't make wise decisions. Here are several examples:

During his reign, he celebrates his wealth and splendor for 180 days. Following this is a weeklong banquet, with an abundance of wine. On the last day, Xerxes—likely under the influence—commands Queen Vashti to come before everyone wearing her crown.

We could understand this command as to be sure to wear her crown. Yet another understanding is that it's a command to wear *only* her crown. This second interpretation would certainly explain why she refuses. Regardless, Xerxes is incensed.

The king asks his aides what to do, and they recommend he depose Vashti. He agrees.

Later, he calms down and remembers what happened. His aides propose an elaborate plan to replace Vashti. He agrees to their suggestion. Out of hundreds of women, possibly thousands, he picks Esther and makes her queen.

In this, we see Xerxes making a rash command while he was drunk. Rather than admit his error, he follows the advice of his aides to deal with the fallout by banishing Vashti. When they recommend a plan to replace her, he agrees even though this will forever negatively impact hundreds of women. But he doesn't care.

Later, Haman—the king's highest official—wants to kill Esther's Uncle Mordecai, along with the rest of the Jews. Haman maneuvers Xerxes into giving him the needed authority. Using the king's signet ring, he issues an edict to kill all the Jews and plunder their property.

Here we see Xerxes giving Haman full authority to act on his behalf. Haman issues an edict designed to cause the death of tens of thousands of Jews throughout the kingdom. But because the king fails to investigate Haman's claims, he's unaware of what's poised to happen.

Fortunately, Esther tactfully brings the situation to Xerxes's attention. Though the edict Haman issued under Xerxes's authorization is irrevocable, a new edict can offset it.

Not learning from his earlier mistake of giving Haman his signet ring, Xerxes now gives it to Mordecai, who issues an edict of his own. Though this protects the Jews from annihilation, it brings about the death of 75,000 others.

Though it's wise to seek advice, how do we know when to not follow the counsel we receive? When have we wrongly given our authority to others?

[Read about Xerxes in Esther 1, Esther 3:10–15, and Esther 8:1–14. Discover more in Daniel 9:1.]

99. JOEL (13)

The Bible mentions fifteen men named Joel, but the prophet Joel is the best known of them all.

From Scripture, it's not possible to place him chronologically, but many Bible scholars view him as a contemporary of Malachi, possibly with overlapping ministries.

Joel addresses the exiles who have returned to Judah from Babylon. His prophecies talk more about locusts than any other prophet. Only the much longer book of Exodus contains more mentions of locusts than the book of Joel.

In the Bible, locusts usually represent widespread destruction for their ability to strip a field of all its foliage and destroy the crop. Such is the case with the locusts in Joel's prophecy.

Perhaps his best-known passage is Joel 2:28–32. In this, the prophet looks forward to the day when all God's people will receive the Holy Spirit. They will prophesy, have supernatural dreams, and see visions.

Peter quotes this passage in his Pentecost message to explain to the people gathering what is happening: Jesus's followers are not drunk. They're filled with the Holy Spirit, just as Joel foresaw (Acts 2:15–16).

How does Joel's prophecy about the Holy Spirit apply to us today? Do we embrace the Holy Spirit's power or dismiss it?

[Read about Joel in Joel 1:1. Discover more in Acts 2:15–21 and Romans 10:13, which quotes Joel 2:32.]

100. MALACHI

The name Malachi occurs only once in the Bible. The reference gives no background information about him. Bible scholars believe he is a contemporary of Joel.

Malachi addresses the exiles who have returned to Judah from Babylon. He talks about the many ways God's people fall short of the Lord's expectations.

Perhaps his most stinging rebuke is that those who do evil are falsely proclaimed as doing what is good in God's eyes. This assessment displeases the Almighty. We too often encounter this same wrong perspective today.

In a parallel passage, Isaiah proclaims woe to such people (Isaiah 5:20). We should do the same.

In what ways does our world today view those who do evil as good? How can we stand strong amid the twisting of God's truth?

[Read about Malachi in Malachi 1:1. Discover more in Luke 7:27 and Romans 9:13, which quotes Malachi 1:2–3.]

MORE OLD TESTAMENT SINNERS AND SAINTS FOR US TODAY

Continuing the mantle of the book *Old Testament Sinners and Saints*, in *More Old Testament Sinners and Saints* we've considered 100 additional Old Testament characters who make mistakes (sinners) and who do good (saints). We can look at their errors to avoid their blunders or to correct our missteps. We can also look at their successes to celebrate what they did well and inspire us to do better.

A more correct understanding of sinners and saints, however, is to acknowledge that by our nature we are all sinners, every one of us. We all fall short of God's Old Testament expectations.

Yet Jesus offers us a better way.

When we repent and follow him, he makes us

right with Father God. He wipes away the punishment our sins deserve. He gives us a clean record. In this way we become saints. This sainthood—our right standing with God—is a gift freely available to all who choose to receive it.

We don't need to change our behavior to earn our salvation—we can't. It's impossible. All we need to do is accept what Jesus offers: his no-strings-attached present that he graciously extends to us.

It's in *response* to this gift that we may later seek to change our behavior as a way of thanking Jesus for the salvation he gives us.

May the Old Testament characters of the Bible inspire us to move forward as we become more like Jesus in response to our salvation through him.

Here are some questions to consider and spur us on:

- *What Bible characters inspired you the most?*
- *Which stories surprised you?*
- *What errors (sins) do you need to repent of and move away from?*
- *What errors (sins) must you guard against, so you don't repeat the same mistakes?*
- *What characteristics from these Old Testament people can you celebrate and imitate?*

- *What characteristics can you aspire to follow so you become more Christlike?*

Contemplate your answers. Seek insight from the Holy Spirit to help you move forward.

May God bless you as you read his Word and apply it to your life each day. May he receive your efforts as an act of worship, and may the world see your life as a powerful witness.

[Discover more in 2 Timothy 3:16–17].

If you liked *More Old Testament Sinners and Saints,* please leave a review online. Your review will help others discover this book and encourage them to read it too. Thank you.

WHICH BOOK DO YOU WANT TO READ NEXT?

Other books in the Bible Character Sketches Series:

- *Women of the Bible*
- *The Friends and Foes of Jesus*
- *Old Testament Sinners and Saints*
- *Heroes and Heavies of the Apocrypha* (coming fall 2024)

For a list of all Peter's books, go to PeterDeHaan.com/books.

FOR SMALL GROUPS, SUNDAY SCHOOL, AND CLASSROOMS

More *Old Testament Sinners and Saints* makes an ideal Bible study discussion guide for small groups, Sunday School, and classrooms. In preparation for the conversation, read the needed chapters during the week.

For example, if you will meet for:

- Twelve weeks, read eight or nine characters each week.
- Sixteen weeks, read six or seven characters each week.
- One year, read two characters each week.

When you get together, discuss the questions at the end of each chapter. The leader can use all the questions to guide this discussion or pick which ones to focus on.

Before beginning the discussion, pray as a group. Ask for Holy Spirit insight and clarity.

As you discuss the questions for each character:

- Look for how their lives can grow your understanding of God.
- Evaluate how their examples can expand your faith.
- Consider what you need to change in how you live your life.
- Ask God to help you apply what you've learned.

May God bless you as your read and study his word.

IF YOU'RE NEW TO THE BIBLE

Each entry in this book contains Bible references. These can guide you if you want to learn more. If you're not familiar with the Bible, here's a brief overview to get you started, give some context, and minimize confusion.

First, the Bible is a collection of works written by various authors over several centuries. Think of the Bible as a diverse anthology of godly communication. It contains historical accounts, poetry, songs, letters of instruction and encouragement, messages from God sent through his representatives, and prophecies.

Most versions of the Bible have sixty-six books grouped into two sections: The Old Testament and the New Testament. The Old Testament contains thirty-nine books that precede and anticipate Jesus. The New Testament includes twenty-seven books and covers Jesus's life and the work of his followers.

The reference notations in the Bible, such as Romans 3:23, are analogous to line numbers in a Shakespearean play. They serve as a study aid. Since the Bible is much longer and more complex than a play, its reference notations are more involved.

As already mentioned, the Bible is an amalgam of books, or sections, such as Genesis, Psalms, John, Acts, or 1 Peter. These are the names given to them, over time, based on the piece's author, audience, or purpose.

In the 1200s, each book was divided into chapters, such as Acts 2 or Psalm 23. In the 1500s, the chapters were further subdivided into verses, such as John 3:16. Let's use this as an example.

The name of the book (John) appears first, followed by the chapter number (3), a colon, and then the verse number (16). Sometimes called a chapter-verse reference notation, this helps people quickly find a specific text regardless of their version of the Bible.

Although the goal was to place these chapter and verse divisions at logical breaks, they sometimes seem arbitrary. Therefore, it's a good practice to read what precedes and follows each passage you're studying since the text before or after it may contain relevant insight into the portion you're exploring.

Here's how to look up a specific passage in the Bible based on its reference: Most Bibles contain a table of contents, which gives the page number for the beginning of each book. Start there. Locate the book you want to read, and turn to that page. Then flip forward to the chapter you want. Last, skim that chapter to locate the specific verse.

If you want to read online, enter the reference into BibleGateway.com or BibleHub.com. Also check out the YouVersion app.

Learn more about the greatest book ever written at ABibleADay.com, which provides a Bible blog, summaries of the books of the Bible, a dictionary of Bible terms, Bible reading plans, and other resources.

DUPLICATE NAMES

As with the book *Old Testament Sinners and Saints*, several people in this book also share their names with other biblical characters. Sometimes these repeated names occur in the same family tree, where the name given to one child is in honor of someone in their lineage. For example, Abraham's grandfather is Nahor (1), and his brother is Nahor (2). Further complicating matters, some people also share names with cities or regions.

To avoid confusion, I've added a numerical suffix to distinguish duplicate names.

Here are the names in this book which are shared with other people in Scripture, with the person we covered in this book in italics.

Abimelek

Abimelek (1), a king during the time of Abraham (Genesis 20:1–2)
Abimelek (2), the son of Gideon (Jerub-Baal) (Judges 9:1)
Abimelek (3), a king during the time of King David (Psalm 34:1)

Adonijah

Adonijah (1), the fourth son of King David (2 Samuel 3:4)
Adonijah (2), a Levite during the reign of King Jehoshaphat (2 Chronicles 17:7–9)
Adonijah (3), a leader during the time of Nehemiah (Nehemiah 10:14–16)

Ahimelek

Ahimelek (1), a priest during the time of King David (1 Samuel 21:1)
Ahimelek (2), a Hittite who was in King David's army (1 Samuel 26:6)

Amasa

Amasa (1), commander over Absalom's army and later for King David (2 Samuel 17:25)
Amasa (2), a leader in Ephraim during the reign of King Ahaz (2 Chronicles 28:12)

Amnon

Amnon (1), King David's firstborn son (2 Samuel 3:2)
Amnon (2), a son of Shimon (1 Chronicles 4:20)

Amos

Amos (1), a prophet (Amos 1:1)
Amos (2), an ancestor of Jesus (Luke 3:25)

Basemath

Basemath (1), one of Esau's wives and daughter of Elon (Genesis 26:34)
Basemath (2), a daughter of Ishmael (Genesis 36:3)
Basemath (3), a daughter of Solomon and wife of Ahimaaz (1 Kings 4:15)

Deborah

Deborah (1), Rebekah's nurse (Genesis 35:8)
Deborah (2), a prophet and judge (Judges 4:4)

Ehud

Ehud (1), a judge (Judges 3:15)
Ehud (2), a son of Bilhan (1 Chronicles 7:10)

Eleazar

Eleazar (1), a son of Aaron and a priest (Exodus 6:23)
Eleazar (2), a son of Abinadab, consecrated to guard the ark (1 Samuel 7:1)
Eleazar (3), a son of Dodai and one of David's mighty warriors (2 Samuel 23:9–10)
Eleazar (4), a son of Mahli (1 Chronicles 23:21)
Eleazar (5), a descendant of Parosh who returned to Judah from captivity (Ezra 10:25)
Eleazar (6), a priest during the time of Nehemiah; he *could* be the same as Eleazar (5) (Nehemiah 12:42)
Eleazar (7), an ancestor of Jesus (Matthew 1:15)

Eliezer

Eliezer (1), the lead servant of Abram (Abraham) (Genesis 15:2)
Eliezer (2), a son of Moses (Exodus 18:2–4)
Eliezer (3), a son of Beker (1 Chronicles 7:8)
Eliezer (4), a priest during the reign of King David (1 Chronicles 15:24)
Eliezer (5), a son of Zikri and tribal leader during the reign of King David (1 Chronicles 27:16)
Eliezer (6), a son of Dodavahu and prophet during the reign of King Jehoshaphat (2 Chronicles 20:37)
Eliezer (7), a leader who returned from captivity with Ezra (Ezra 8:16)
Eliezer (8), a priest guilty of marrying a foreign woman (Ezra 10:18)
Eliezer (9), a Levite guilty of marrying a foreign woman (Ezra 10:23)
Eliezer (10), a descendant of Harim guilty of marrying a foreign woman (Ezra 10:31)
Eliezer (11), an ancestor of Jesus (Luke 3:29)

Elkanah

Elkanah (1), a son of Korah (Exodus 6:24)

Elkanah (2), a son or descendant of Elkanah (1) (1 Chronicles 6:26)
Elkanah (3), another descendant of Elkanah (1) (1 Chronicles 6:27)
Elkanah (4), the husband of Hannah (1 Samuel 1:1–2)
Elkanah (5), one of King David's warriors (1 Chronicles 12:6)
Elkanah (6), doorkeeper of the ark during the reign of King David (1 Chronicles 15:23)
Elkanah (7), an official under King Ahaz (2 Chronicles 28:7)
Elkanah (8), an ancestor of Berekiah (1 Chronicles 9:16)

Enoch

Enoch (1), son of Adam and Eve's son Cain (Genesis 4:17)
Enoch (2), a descendant of Adam and Eve's son Seth and ancestor of Jesus (Genesis 5:21–24)

Er

Er (1), firstborn son of Judah and first husband to Tamar (1) (Genesis 38:1–7)

Er (2), an ancestor of Jesus (Luke 3:28)

Gershom

Gershom (1), a son of Moses (Exodus 2:22)
Gershom (2), a family head who returned to Judah with Ezra (Ezra 8:1–2)

Gomer

Gomer (1), a son of Japheth (Genesis 10:2)
Gomer (2), wife of Hosea (Hosea 1:2–3)

Joel

Joel (1), firstborn son of Samuel (1 Samuel 8:2)
Joel (2), a descendant of Simeon and clan leader (1 Chronicles 4:35–38)
Joel (3), a descendant of Reuben (1 Chronicles 5:1–4)
Joel (4), another descendant of Reuben (1 Chronicles 5:7–8)
Joel (5), a descendant of Gad (1 Chronicles 5:12)
Joel (6), ancestor of a temple musician during the reign of King David (1 Chronicles 6:33)

Joel (7), another ancestor of a temple musician during the reign of King David (1 Chronicles 6:36)

Joel (8), a descendant of Issachar and son of Izrahiah (1 Chronicles 7:1–3)

Joel (9), one of David's mighty warriors (1 Chronicles 11:38)

Joel (10), a descendant of Gershon during the reign of King David (1 Chronicles 15:7)

Joel (11), a leader over the half-tribe of Manasseh during the reign of King David (1 Chronicles 27:20)

Joel (12), a Levite during the reign of King Hezekiah (2 Chronicles 29:12)

Joel (13), the prophet (Joel 1:1)

Joel (14), a gatekeeper guilty of marrying a foreign woman (Ezra 10:43)

Joel (15), a descendant of Benjamin who settled in Jerusalem during the time of Nehemiah (Nehemiah 11:7–9)

Josiah

Josiah (1), son of King Amon and king of Judah (2 Kings 22:1)

Josiah (2), son of Zephaniah (1) (Zechariah 6:10)

Jotham

Jotham (1), son of Gideon (Jerub-Baal) (Judges 9:5)
Jotham (2), a descendant of Caleb (1 Chronicles 2:47)
Jotham (3), a king of Judah (2 Kings 15:5–7)

Korah

Korah (1), a son of Esau (Genesis 36:14)
Korah (2), a descendant of Esau, through Eliphaz (Genesis 36:15–16)
Korah (3), a great-grandson (or descendant) of Levi who opposed Moses (Numbers 16:1–6)
Korah (4), a descendant of Caleb (1 Chronicles 2:42–43)
Korah (5), a descendant of Korah (3) (1 Chronicles 9:17–19)

Lamech

Lamech (1), a descendant of Cain (Genesis 4:17–18)
Lamech (2), son of Methuselah, father of Noah, and ancestor of Jesus (Genesis 5:25–31)

Micah

Micah (1), a man in the book of Judges, though arguably not a judge (Judges 17:1)
Micah (2), a descendant of Reuben (1 Chronicles 5:1–5)
Micah (3), a great-grandson of King Saul (1 Chronicles 8:33–34)
Micah (4), a grandson of Kohath and cousin of Moses (1 Chronicles 23:12 & 20)
Micah (5), a prophet from Moresheth (Micah 1:1)

Nadab

Nadab (1), a son of Aaron (Exodus 6:23)
Nadab (2), a great-uncle of King Saul (1 Chronicles 9:35–39)
Nadab (3), son of Jeroboam and a king of Israel (1 Kings 14:19–20)

Nahor

Nahor (1), grandfather of Abram (Abraham) (Genesis 11:22–26)
Nahor (2), brother of Abram (Abraham) (Genesis 11:27)

Nahum

Nahum (1), a prophet (Nahum 1:1)
Nahum (2), an ancestor of Jesus (Luke 3:23–25)

Nathan

Nathan (1), a son of King David (2 Samuel 5:13–14)
Nathan (2), a prophet during the time of King David (2 Samuel 7:1–4)
Nathan (3), one of King David's mighty warriors (2 Samuel 23:36)
Nathan (4), a descendant of Judah and Caleb (1 Chronicles 2:36)
Nathan (5), a leader who returned from captivity with Ezra (Ezra 8:16)
Nathan (6), a man guilty of marrying a foreign woman (Ezra 10:38–39)

Obadiah

Obadiah (1), a descendant of Issachar (1 Chronicles 7:1–3)

More Old Testament Sinners and Saints

Obadiah (2), a warrior who defected to join David (1 Chronicles 12:8–9)

Obadiah (3), a descendant of King Saul (1 Chronicles 8:38)

Obadiah (4), a palace administrator for King Ahab and devoted believer (1 Kings 18:3–4)

Obadiah (5), an official of King Jehoshaphat (2 Chronicles 17:7)

Obadiah (6), a Levite who supervised laborers when King Josiah repaired the temple (2 Chronicles 34:12)

Obadiah (7), a descendant of King Jehoiachin (1 Chronicles 3:17–21)

Obadiah (8), a prophet (Obadiah 1:1)

Obadiah (9), a Levite, son of Shemaiah, who returns to Judah from captivity (1 Chronicles 9:14–16)

Obadiah (10), a Levite, son of Jehiel, who returns to Judah with Ezra (Ezra 8:9)

Obadiah (11), a priest under Governor Nehemiah (Nehemiah 10:1–8)

Obadiah (12), a gatekeeper who guarded the storerooms during the time of Nehemiah and Ezra (Nehemiah 12:25–26)

Obed

Obed (1), the son of Ruth and Boaz and the grandfather of King David (Ruth 4:13–17)
Obed (2), one of King David's mighty warriors (1 Chronicles 11:47)
Obed (3), a gatekeeper during the reign of King David (1 Chronicles 26:7)
Obed (4), a descendant of Judah (1 Chronicles 2:37–38)

Phinehas

Phinehas (1), a grandson of Aaron (Exodus 6:25)
Phinehas (2), a son of Eli (1 Samuel 1:3)
Phinehas (3), father of Eleazar (5) (Ezra 8:33)

Puah

Puah (1), a son of Issachar (Genesis 46:13)
Puah (2), a Hebrew midwife in Egypt (Exodus 1:15–21)

Reuel

Reuel (1), a son of Esau (Genesis 36:10)
Reuel (2), Moses's father-in-law and later called Jethro (Numbers 10:29)
Reuel (3), a descendant of Benjamin (1 Chronicles 9:7–9)

Shelah

Shelah (1), a descendant of Noah's son Shem (Genesis 10:21–24)
Shelah (2), an ancestor of Abraham and of Jesus (Luke 3:35)
Shelah (3), a son of Judah (Genesis 38:1–5)

Sons of Korah

Sons of Korah (1), Korah (Moses's cousin) has three sons: Assir, Elkanah, and Abiasaph (Exodus 6:24)
Sons of Korah (2), psalm writers or performers during the time of King David (Psalm 42:1)

Tamar

Tamar (1), the daughter-in-law of Judah and mother of his twins (Genesis 38:6–30)
Tamar (2), sister of Absalom (2 Samuel 13:1–22)
Tamar (3), daughter of Absalom (2 Samuel 14:27)

Zadok

Zadok (1), a priest during the time of King David (2 Samuel 8:15–17)
Zadok (2), grandfather of King Jotham (2 Chronicles 27:1)
Zadok (3), son of Baana, who helped rebuild the fallen wall in Jerusalem (Nehemiah 3:1–4)
Zadok (4), son of Immer, who also helped rebuild the fallen wall in Jerusalem (Nehemiah 3:29)
Zadok (5), a leader of the people during the time of Governor Nehemiah, possibly Zadok (3) or (4) (Nehemiah 10:21)
Zadok (6), a scribe during the time of Governor Nehemiah, possibly Zadok (3) or (4) (Nehemiah 13:13)
Zadok (7), an ancestor of Jesus (Matthew 1:14)

Zechariah

Zechariah (1), king of Israel (2 Kings 14:29)
Zechariah (2), a descendant of Reuben
(1 Chronicles 5:7–8)
Zechariah (3), the gatekeeper and son of
Meshelemiah (1 Chronicles 9:21 and 1 Chronicles 26:1–2)
Zechariah (4), a descendant of Saul (1 Chronicles 9:37 and possibly 1 Chronicles 15:18)
Zechariah (5), a musician (1 Chronicles 15:20)
Zechariah (6), a priest (1 Chronicles 15:24)
Zechariah (7), a Levite during the time of King David (1 Chronicles 16:5)
Zechariah (8), another gatekeeper and son of Hosah (1 Chronicles 26:10–11)
Zechariah (9), a third gatekeeper, a wise counselor, and son of Shelemiah (1 Chronicles 26:14)
Zechariah (10), father of Iddo during the time of King David (1 Chronicles 27:21)
Zechariah (11), an official of King Jehoshaphat (2 Chronicles 17:7) and possibly his son (2 Chronicles 21:2)
Zechariah (12), son of Jehoiada the priest (2 Chronicles 24:20)

Zechariah (13), a king of Judah and grandfather of King Hezekiah (2 Chronicles 29:1)

Zechariah (14), an official of King Josiah (2 Chronicles 35:8)

Zechariah (15), the prophet and a descendant of Iddo (Ezra 5:1, the book of Zechariah, and possibly Ezra 8:3)

Zechariah (16), a priest guilty of marrying a foreign woman (Ezra 10:26)

Zechariah (17), son of Amariah and father of Uzziah (Nehemiah 11:4)

Zechariah (18), father of Joiarib and descendant of Zechariah (16) (Nehemiah 11:5)

Zechariah (19), son of Jonathan (Nehemiah 12:35)

Zechariah (20), a reliable witness and son of Jeberekiah (Isaiah 8:2)

Zechariah (21), son of Berekiah, who was murdered between the temple and the altar (Matthew 23:35)

Zechariah (22), the husband of Elizabeth and father of John the Baptist (Luke 1:5–25 and Luke 1:57–66)

[With the number of obscure mentions of Zechariah throughout the Bible—fifty-nine times in nine books—it's impossible to determine accurately how many there are, but there are many. The main ones are Zechariah (1), the king of Israel; Zechariah (15), the prophet; and Zechariah (22), the father of

More Old Testament Sinners and Saints

John the Baptist. The preceding listing is reasonable but not absolute.]

Zephaniah

Zephaniah (1), a prophet and son of Cushi (Zephaniah 1:1)
Zephaniah (2), a Levite and son of Tahath (1 Chronicles 6:36–37)
Zephaniah (3), a priest and son of Maaseiah during the time of Jeremiah (Jeremiah 29:25)
Zephaniah (4), a priest during the reign of King Zedekiah and taken captive when King Nebuchadnezzar conquered Jerusalem. He could be Zephaniah (2), Zephaniah (3), or a different Zephaniah altogether (2 Kings 25:18)

Zerah

Zerah (1), a grandson of Esau (Genesis 36:13)
Zerah (2), the father of Johab, who ruled Edom (Genesis 36:31–33)
Zerah (3), one of the twins born to Tamar (1) and Judah (Genesis 38:27–30)
Zerah (4), another descendant of Judah (Joshua 7:18)

Zerah (5), a descendant of Simeon (1 Chronicles 4:24)

Zerah (6), a descendant of Levi (1 Chronicles 6:20–21)

Zerah (7), a Cushite military leader who opposed King Asa (2 Chronicles 14:9–10)

ABOUT PETER DEHAAN

Peter DeHaan, PhD, wants to change the world one word at a time. His books and blog posts discuss God, the Bible, and church, geared toward spiritual seekers and church dropouts. Many people feel church has let them down, and Peter seeks to encourage them as they search for a place to belong.

But he's not afraid to ask tough questions or make religious people squirm. He's not trying to be provocative. Instead, he seeks truth, even if it makes people uncomfortable. Peter urges Christians to push past the status quo and reexamine how they practice their faith in every part of their lives.

Peter earned his doctorate, awarded with high distinction, from Trinity College of the Bible and

Theological Seminary. He lives with his wife in beautiful Southwest Michigan and wrangles crossword puzzles in his spare time.

Peter's a lifelong student of Scripture. He wrote the 1,000-page website ABibleADay.com to encourage people to explore the Bible, the greatest book ever written. His popular blog addresses biblical Christianity to build a faith that matters.

Read his blog, receive his newsletter, and learn more at PeterDeHaan.com.

PETER DEHAAN'S BOOKS

Bible Character Sketches Series:

Women of the Bible

The Friends and Foes of Jesus

Old Testament Sinners and Saints

More Old Testament Sinners and Saints

Heroes and Heavies of the Apocrypha (fall 2024)

Holiday Celebration Bible Study Series:

The Advent of Jesus (an Advent devotional)

The Ministry of Jesus (an Ordinary Time devotional)

The Passion of Jesus (a Lenten devotional)

The Victory of Jesus (an Easter devotional)

40-Day Bible Study Series:

That You May Know (the Gospel of Luke)

Tongues of Fire (the book of Acts)

For Unto Us (the prophet Isaiah)

Return to Me (the Minor Prophets)

I Hope in Him (the book of Job)

Living Water (the Gospel of John)

Love Is Patient (Paul's letters to the Corinthians)

A New Heaven and a New Earth (John's Revelation)

Love One Another (John's letters)

Run with Perseverance (the book of Hebrews)

Visiting Churches Series:

Shopping for Church

Visiting Online Church

52 Churches

The 52 Churches Workbook

More Than 52 Churches

The More Than 52 Churches Workbook

Other Books:

Jesus's Broken Church

Martin Luther's 95 Theses

The Christian Church's LGBTQ Failure

Bridging the Sacred-Secular Divide

Beyond Psalm 150

How Big Is Your Tent?

For the latest list of all Peter's books, go to PeterDeHaan.com/books.

www.ingramcontent.com/pod-product-compliance
Lightning Source LLC
Chambersburg PA
CBHW050244010526
44107CB00003B/178